# BIG
# ENGLISH 5

Mario Herrera

Christopher Sol Cruz

**PUPIL'S BOOK**

# Contents

| CLIL | Writing | Life Skills/Project | Phonics | I can... |
|---|---|---|---|---|
| **Science:** The two sides of the brain<br>analyse, brain, control, creative, instructions, personality, solve<br>**Additional language:** Compound adjectives<br>**Sports for All Times:** Early Olympic events<br>competition, medals, metres, Olympic Games, race course, sporting events | News article | **Be a team player.**<br>Talk about working together.<br>Make a poster to find new members of a team, club or group. | **ce, ci, cir**<br>cell, centre<br>cinema, city<br>circle, circus | ...make suggestions.<br>...talk about my interests. |
| **Science:** Animal mothers<br>offspring, predator, protect, young (n.)<br>**Special Days for Families:** Traditions around the world<br>celebrate, decorate, holiday, special, traditions, wedding<br>**Additional language:** Quantity: *some, many, a lot of, all* | Autobiography | **Keep family traditions.**<br>Talk about family traditions.<br>Make a class book about family traditions. | **ge, gi, gy**<br>gel, gem<br>ginger, giraffe<br>gym, gypsy | ...talk about important life events that happened in the past.<br>...make comparisons. |
| **Art:** How to create an effective poster or advert; advert designs<br>advertisement, design, effective, font, images, layout<br>**Additional language:** Zero conditionals with *if*<br>**Doing What You Can:** Children who help others<br>animal rescue, benefit (v.), charity groups, donate, homeless, tutoring | Letter | **Help others.**<br>Talk about international charities.<br>Write a fundraising plan and create an advert for an event. | **lk, mb**<br>chalk, talk, walk<br>climb, comb, lamb | ...talk about helping others and about fundraising activities.<br>...talk about possibilities.<br>...say what I'm going to do. |
| **History:** The history of money<br>bronze, coins, grain, livestock, metal, paper money, shells, trade<br>**Additional language:** Prepositions: *during, over, until*<br>**Shop till you Drop:** Famous places around the world for shopping<br>crafts, traditional, vendor | Product review | **Develop good money habits.**<br>Talk about what you do with your money.<br>Design a shopping bag that encourages good spending habits. | **sc, ho**<br>muscle, scene, science<br>echo, ghost, honest | ...talk about shopping.<br>...make comparisons. |
| **Maths:** Buying things for a holiday; find totals for items bought<br>addition, customer, item, multiplication, realise, total<br>**Additional language:** *need to, needn't*<br>**Unique Holiday Destinations:** Strange places for holidays<br>destinations, expedition, frozen, igloo, overnight, tour | Postcards | **Be safe on holiday.**<br>Talk about holidays and safety tips.<br>Make a holiday safety poster. | **cl, tw**<br>clap, clock, clown<br>twelve, twist, twin | ...talk about holiday problems.<br>...talk about what was going on when something happened. |
| **Science:** How robots help us<br>assistive, gestures, procedures, robotic, socially, surgical<br>**Endangered Languages:** Three languages that are almost extinct<br>dialect, endangered, extinct, speaking | Diary entry | **Have dreams for the future.**<br>Talk about future dreams.<br>Design an advert for a product or service in the future. | **pp, bb, dd, mm, nn, tt**<br>happy<br>hobby<br>ladder<br>summer<br>tennis<br>butter | ...make predictions about the future.<br>...talk about technology. |
| **Social Science:** Important inventions<br>candle, cash register, combustion engine, fuel, organise, plumbing<br>**Cool Transformations:** How designers have changed everyday objects<br>aquarium, helmet, hollow, log, protect, transform | Description: Object | **Appreciate history.**<br>Talk about your culture and learn the importance of appreciating history.<br>Make a class book about items from different cultures. | **lt, lk, ld, lb**<br>belt<br>milk, silk<br>cold, field<br>bulb | ...guess what things are or might be.<br>...say what things are used for or used to do. |
| **Science:** How fresh produce travels<br>diesel fuel, distribution centre, local, pollution, produce, typical<br>**Additional language:** Conjunction: *so*<br>**Where Did It Come From?:** Where foods and products originally came from<br>century, chemicals, explorer, factory, fire, phosphorus, sulphur | Persuasive writing | **Appreciate what you eat and use every day.**<br>Talk about things you appreciate and where they come from.<br>Make a poster about things you appreciate and where they come from. | **lf, lp, lm**<br>elf, golf<br>help<br>elm, film | ...talk about where goods come from.<br>...talk about products and the materials used to make them.<br>...use the passive voice. |
| **Science:** The effects of adrenalin on the body<br>adrenal glands, adrenalin, cells, heart, hormone, lungs, release, stress<br>**High Adventure!:** Risky activities<br>aerialist, centimetre, extreme, metre, parachute, rescue, risk | Description: Experience | **Explore your surroundings.**<br>To learn the value of exploring your surroundings.<br>Make a collage about things to explore in your community. | **ft, ct, mp, sk**<br>left, raft<br>fact<br>camp, lamp<br>risk | ...talk about experiences.<br>...talk about preferences. |

# unit 1 MY INTERESTS

**1:04**

**1** Read about these famous people. What were they interested in? Complete the sentences with a word from the box. Then listen and check.

> computer    football    mathematics    money    music

1 Growing up, actor Antonio Banderas was interested in sports like 🔢 . He played for his school team. When he was 14, he broke his foot, ending his dreams of a professional sporting career.

2 One of the richest people in the world, Carlos Slim was interested in managing his 🔢 at a young age. He bought shares in his first bank when he was just 12 years old.

3 World-famous scientist Albert Einstein was interested in 🔢 as a boy. He played the violin and the piano.

4 Actress Emma Stone always wanted to act. She was also good at using a 🔢 . When she was 14, she used a PowerPoint presentation to convince her parents to let her begin a career in acting.

5 As a young woman, architect and artist Maya Lin loved bird-watching, hiking and studying 🔢 .

**2** Match the names of the school groups to the pictures. Then listen and check.

> basketball team    drama club    school newspaper
> school orchestra    science club    tae kwon do club

1

2

3

4

5

6

**3** Read. Look at 2. Which school group should each pupil join?

1 Dan loves jogging and playing sports. He's got a lot of free time.

2 Dina loves acting. Someday, she would like to star in a film.

3 Milan is good at writing and has got his own blog.

4 Paul likes martial arts and is very athletic. He likes playing chess, too.

5 Jane is interested in building robots. She's good at Science and Maths.

6 Sara likes playing the trumpet. She's good at it, too.

**4** Work with a partner. Ask and answer.

What's Dan interested in doing?

Which school group should he join?

He's interested in jogging and playing sports.

The basketball team!

**THINK BIG** Which activities could you still do as an adult? Have adults got similar interests to young people? Why/Why not?

1:07

**5** Listen and read. When are the football team try-outs?

| Home | School Library | Cafeteria Menu | For Parents |

# The Grove School News

## GET BUSY AFTER SCHOOL!

Welcome back to school! From all the staff here at your school news blog, we hope you're ready for another great year. Have you signed up for an after-school activity yet? If not, don't worry! There's still time. Here are some of the activities you can try:

Tony Underwood scoring the winning goal at last year's county championships

### SPORTS TEAMS

Do you like sports? How about joining the football or athletics team? Both teams have try-outs next Monday and Tuesday at 3:00. Last year, our school football team won the county championships but many of our best players have moved up to secondary school. So now the team needs new players. For more information, contact our sports advisors, Ms Matte or Mr Stergis.

Sam Penny showing his artistic talents

### GOOD AT ART?

This year, your classmates in the school art club plan to paint a mural on the wall by the office. So they need new members to help create it! Are you interested in drawing, painting or taking photographs? This club is for you. The first meeting of the school year is next Wednesday at 3:15 in room 221. Please see Ms Greenway for more information.

## NEW THIS YEAR

There are some new activities you can have a go at. Try the new after-school science club! It has plans to enter the national Junior Robotics competition this year. So if you want to try building a robot, this club is for you. See Mr Larson in room 105 for more details. The club meets every Thursday.

Do you like acting? Are you good at singing? The school play this year is a musical – *The Sound of Music*. Come and try out next Monday or Wednesday afternoon in the school auditorium. Sign-up sheets for auditions are on the wall outside room 125.

For a list of all the after-school activities this year, click here. Or pick up a membership form from the advisor's office – room 103.

### Comments

**dharrison**
Don't forget the karate club! We need members, too! Anyone interested in joining should contact Mr Silver.

**agrell**
Robots? Cool! Count me in!

**apritchett**
Acting in the school play was so much fun last year. And I love singing. I want to try out again!

## READING COMPREHENSION

**6** Answer the questions with a partner.

1 Which school team won a big competition last year?

2 Where can you get more information about the science club?

3 When are the auditions for the school play?

4 What's the art club planning to do this year?

5 Where can you find a complete list of all the after-school activities?

**THINK BIG** Which activities in the article interest you? Why? Are you interested in doing any of your school's activities or joining any clubs? Why/Why not?

# Language in Action

**7** Listen and read. What's Henry good at? Practise the dialogue with a partner.

**Ms Parks:** Henry, I was wondering. Are you interested in joining a club this year?

**Henry:** I am but I'm not sure which one to join.

**Ms Parks:** How about joining the science club? You're good at building things.

**Henry:** Maybe… When do they meet?

**Ms Parks:** Every Monday after school.

**Henry:** Oh, I can't. I've got guitar lessons on Mondays.

**Ms Parks:** OK. Well, how about joining the art club?

**Henry:** The art club?

**Ms Parks:** Yes. You're so good at drawing. And they meet on Tuesdays.

**Henry:** Tuesdays are fine for me. I think I'll do it.

**8** Practise the dialogue in 7 with a partner.

**9** Listen and match the after-school activities to the timetables. Then say what each pupil is interested in.

acting    playing football    reading comics    writing    busy = ■

   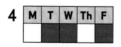

| How about **joining** the drama club? | No, thanks. I'm not good at **acting**. |
|---|---|
| How about **trying out** for the basketball team? | OK. I love **playing** basketball. |

**Tip:** Use the gerund form of the verb (verb + *ing*) after *How about, love, like, enjoy, be interested in* and *be good at*.

**10** **Use the words to help you make questions.**

1 football team/try out

2 school newspaper/join

3 school musical/try out

4 English club/join

5 school orchestra/try out

6 hiking club/join

**11** **Complete the sentences with the correct form of the verb in brackets.**

1 No, thanks. I'm not very good at 🎱 . (sing)

2 Sounds great. I'm really interested in 🎱 more English. (learn)

3 Good idea. I love 🎱 the violin. (play)

4 Why not? I like 🎱 football a lot. (play)

5 Oh, no! I don't enjoy 🎱 at all. (walk)

6 I don't think so. I'm not interested in 🎱 articles. (write)

**12** **Match the questions and answers in 10 and 11. Practise the dialogues with a partner. Then take turns asking and answering the questions again with your own answers.**

How about trying out for the football team?

I don't think so. I'm...

1:13

**13** Listen and read. Which side of your brain might be stronger if you're good at remembering people's names?

CONTENT WORDS

analyse   brain   control   creative   instructions   personality   solve

# Left Brained or Right Brained?

Left-brained people are good at analysing details. They enjoy doing things like solving Maths problems and playing chess.

Right-brained people are creative. They're good at things like painting, playing music and acting. Some people are left brained *and* right brained!

Did you know that what you're good at doing might have something to do with your brain? The brain's got two sides: the left brain and the right brain. Some scientists believe that each side of the brain controls different parts of our personality and that each person has got one side that's stronger. That stronger side may help determine, in some ways, what we like to do, what we're good at and what we're interested in.

## Which side of your brain is stronger?

Take this short quiz. Choose (A) or (B) to answer each question.

1   Do you prefer going to (A) Maths lessons or (B) Art lessons?

2   Do you like (A) planning everything or (B) not planning at all?

3   Do you like (A) a lot of instructions or (B) not many instructions?

4   Do you remember things more easily (A) with words or (B) with pictures?

5   When you meet people, do you remember (A) their name or (B) their face?

6   When you read a story, do you look for (A) details or (B) the big picture?

How did you score? If you have more As, the left side of your brain may be stronger. If you have more Bs, the right side is probably stronger. Now think about the kinds of activities you like to do. Do they match your brain type?

**14** Read 13 again and say left brained or right brained.

1   He's really good at drawing.

2   She likes following detailed instructions.

3   I write something down to remember it.

THINK BIG
Which activities do you think are better for a left-brained person? Which activities are better for a right-brained person?

1:14

**15** Listen and read. In what year was skijoring an Olympic sport?

# Sports for All Times

One of the world's most popular sporting events, the Olympics, is older than you might think. It started almost 3,000 years ago, around 776 BC.

Some of the early Olympic events are the same ones we see today. But other Olympic events were just too strange or not popular enough to stay. Take a look at these.

### Skijoring

The name *skijoring* means 'ski-driving' in Norwegian. In this sport, a horse pulls a person on skis over a race course covered in snow! This strange sport from Norway was part of the Olympics only once, in 1928.

### Hot Air Ballooning

During the Paris Olympics of 1900, hot air ballooning was introduced to the Olympic Games. Players competed to see how far and high they could go. French competitors won every time!

### Tug-of-War

Did you know that in 1900, 1904, 1908, 1912 and 1920, tug-of-war was a regular Olympic event? The Olympic tug-of-war competition had eight players at each end of a long rope. The team that pulled the other team 2 metres won the event. In the five years of this Olympic game, Great Britain won the most tug-of-war medals.

**16** Read 15 again and match.

| | |
|---|---|
| **1** hot air ballooning | **a** how fast |
| **2** tug-of-war | **b** how strong |
| **3** skijoring | **c** how far and how high |

**17** Read the article. Then study the questions and answers below.

### The Grove School News

Our school science club went to the national Junior Robotics Competition last month. The competition took place at the Science Museum in London. The science club won fifth place. We're very proud of our science club! All of the students in it are good at designing and building robots. We're sure they'll be happy to show you the award-winning robots. Just ask any member of the science club.

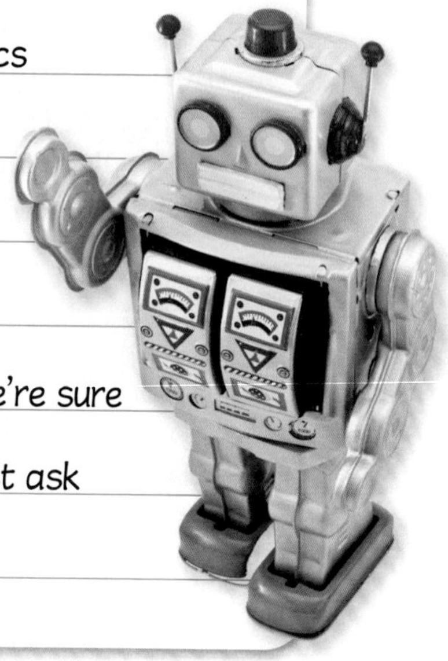

| When? | What happened? |
|---|---|
| 1  Who? | school science club |
| 2  What? | national Junior Robotics Competition |
| 3  Where? | Science Museum, London |
| 4  When? | last month |
| 5  What happened? | they won fifth place |

**18** Prepare a news article about a club, team or group at your school. Copy the chart above into your notebook and answer the questions to help you gather information.

**19** Display your articles on a school noticeboard or use them to put together a school newspaper of your own.

**THINK BIG** Apart from a school newspaper, what else could you write articles for?

**20** Which person in each picture is not being a team player? How can that person become a team player? Discuss with a partner.

1   2   3

 He needs to pass the ball!

I agree.

**21** Are you a team player? Discuss with a partner. When do you need to work in a team? Give three examples.

## PROJECT

**22** Make a poster to find new members for a club, team or group at your school.

**1:15**

**23** Listen, read and repeat.

**1** c-e   ce          **2** c-i   ci          **3** c-ir   cir

 **1:16**

**24** Listen and blend the sounds.

**1** c-e-ll          cell          **2** c-i-t-y          city

**3** c-ir-c-u-s          circus          **4** c-i-n-e-m-a          cinema

**5** c-e-n-tre          centre          **6** c-ir-c-le          circle

 **1:17**

**25** Listen and chant.

Have fun in the city!
Go to the cinema.
Have fun in the city!
Go to the centre.

 **1:18**

**26** Work with a partner. Read the directions, listen to the model and play.

**1** Partner A numbers the School Club or Group Cards from 1–6 in any order in their notebook. Partner B numbers the Interest Cards from 1–6 in any order.

**2** Partner A makes a suggestion and Partner B answers, using an Interest Card with the same number.

**3** If Partner B's interests don't match Partner A's suggestion, Partner A offers another suggestion. Partners cross out each card in their notebook as it is used.

**School Club or Group Cards**

 chess club

 school orchestra / drama club

 school newspaper / football team

 tae kwon do club

**Interest Cards**

 sing

 play board games / do martial arts / play the trumpet / play sports

write

**27** Match the activities to the correct groups.

1 school newspaper
2 school orchestra
3 tae kwon do club
4 art club
5 science club

a building robots
b writing articles
c drawing
d playing a musical instrument
e painting
f taking photos
g doing martial arts

**28** Complete the dialogue with words from the box. Use the correct verb form.

do    join    play    sign up    try out    write

**John:** What do you do after school? Are you in any school clubs this year?

**Sally:** No, but I'm thinking about ¹ 🔒 for one.

**John:** Well, how about the gymnastics club? You're interested in ² 🔒 gymnastics, aren't you?

**Sally:** That's true but I haven't got time for that club. They practise five days a week.

**John:** How about ³ 🔒 for the basketball team?

**Sally:** I'm not really interested in ⁴ 🔒 sports right now.

**John:** Really? Well, do you like ⁵ 🔒 .

**Sally:** Yes, I do.

**John:** Then how about ⁶ 🔒 the school news bloggers? They always need people. And blogging doesn't take up that much time!

**Sally:** Hmm… good idea. I might just do that.

**I Can**

• **make suggestions.**

• **talk about my interests.**

# unit 2 FAMILY TIES

1:19

**1** Read and answer the questions about families. Then listen and check.

**1 How Many Mackenzies?**

Mr and Mrs Mackenzie have six daughters and each daughter has one brother. How many people are in the Mackenzie family?

**2 Family Name Trivia**

What's the most common family name in the world: Chang, García or Smith?

**3 Big Families**

Which country has got the largest average household size: Italy, Canada or Colombia?

**4 Good Grief, Grandma!**

Bai Ulan Kudanding, a woman in the southern Philippines, has 14 children, 107 grandchildren, 138 great-grandchildren and two great-great-grandchildren. She knows all of their names! How many children are there in all?

**2** Listen and find the family members in the photos. Use words from the box to name them.

**Calderon Family**

| | | |
|---|---|---|
| me | my aunt and uncle | my baby sister |
| my dad | my mum | my older brother |

1

2

3

4

**3** Copy the chart into your notebook. Listen again and complete the chart.

| What? | Who? | Where? | When? |
|---|---|---|---|
| **1** moved | Andrea, her older brother Pedro and their mum and dad | Brighton | 2012 |
| **2** opened a restaurant | | | |
| **3** was born | | | |
| **4** got married | | ~ | ~ |
| **5** graduated from cooking school | | | |

**4** Work with a partner. Ask and answer about the Calderon family.

When was her baby sister born?

She was born in 2013.

**THINK BIG** What challenges can you think of for a family moving to a new country?

**5** Listen and read. How many Flying Maliceks are there now?

# The Biggest Circus Family
# IN THE WORLD
## by Zach Malicek

My name's Zach and I'm from a big family. I mean, it's a *really* big family. My last name is Malicek. Maybe you don't know us but we're the biggest circus family in the world. We're The Flying Maliceks! We weren't always the biggest circus act, though. When my Grandpa Viktor started as a trapeze performer in Slovakia, there was only one Flying Malicek: him!

My grandpa moved to the United Kingdom when he was about 20 years old. He quickly found a circus job working in his new country. A few years later, Grandpa Viktor married my Grandma Irina. Grandpa taught my grandma how to perform on the trapeze and soon there were two Flying Maliceks. My grandma didn't perform all the time, though. She took time off to have a few babies. She had eight of them, actually!

My father Daniel is the youngest child in the family. He has five brothers and two sisters – my uncles and aunts. And all of them learnt to perform on the trapeze when they were children. The people at the circus love watching the Flying Maliceks. And we all love watching their excited faces when we fly through the air.

My grandpa and grandma are getting older now. They retired from performing about five years ago. But the Flying Maliceks are not getting smaller – we're getting bigger! I have two older sisters and we all perform in the act. My aunts and uncles all have children; and they perform, too. In total there are 37 of us! Can you believe it?

Last year, we were on TV. We had our own reality show called *Circus Family*. Some people from the TV show followed us around with cameras all the time. It was exciting but sometimes I wanted them to go away! One special thing happened when we were on that show. My cousin Gillian met a cameraman and six months ago they got married. Now he's learning the trapeze, too!

## READING COMPREHENSION

**6** Complete the sentences with the correct numbers.

1 Viktor moved to the United Kingdom when he was 🔞 years old.

2 Zach's father is the youngest of 🔞 children.

3 Zach has got 🔞 uncles and 🔞 aunts.

4 Zach has got 🔞 older sisters.

5 Gillian got married 🔞 months ago.

 **THINK BIG** Why do you think the Flying Maliceks are getting bigger?
How many people are there in a 'big' family?
What are the good things about being part of a big family?

# Language in Action

**7** Listen and read. What does Darren learn about Amelia?

**Darren:** Who's that?

**Amelia:** Oh, that's my older brother Armando. That was a long time ago. I think he was about 12 in that photo.

**Darren:** Oh, do you have an older brother?

**Amelia:** Yes. He's a lot older than I am. He's 25. He lives in London.

**Darren:** Really?

**Amelia:** Yes. He moved to London when he was 23. He works in a hotel.

**Darren:** That's nice. Mmm… you look like him… a little bit.

**Amelia:** Do you think so? Maybe. But he's really tall now. Actually, he's about six feet tall. He's the tallest person in our family.

**8** Practise the dialogue in 7 with a partner.

**9** Listen and match. Then say. Use the correct form of a verb from the box.

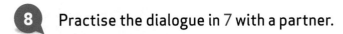

be born    get married    graduate    move

1  She ？        2  They ？        3  I ？        4  We ？

a          b          c          d

> We went to Edinburgh **when I was eight**.
> **When they were children**, they lived in Manchester.
>
> She moved to Cambridge **three years ago**.
> **A few months later**, she got a new job.
>
> **Tip:** Look for signal words like *when, later* and *ago*.

| Present simple | → | Past simple |
|---|---|---|
| go | → | went |
| am | → | was |
| are | → | were |
| live | → | lived |
| get | → | got |
| move | → | moved |

**10** Complete the paragraph. Use the correct form of the verbs.

This is my older sister Lisa. She's very happy today because, a few hours ago, she ¹ 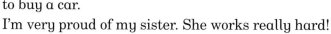 (buy) her first car! She saved money from all her part-time jobs. She ² (get) her first job a long time ago when she ³ (be) only 11 years old. She delivered newspapers in our neighbourhood. Later, when she was 14, she ⁴ (start) to tutor younger children after school. Then, when Lisa was 16, she ⁵ (find) a job at a restaurant. She ⁶ (work) there almost every weekend when she was in the sixth form. Then, a week ago, she finally ⁷ (have) enough money to buy a car.
I'm very proud of my sister. She works really hard!

> Sue's **taller than** Yoko and Mark.
>
> Sue's **the tallest** person in our class.

**11** Look at the pictures and make sentences.

**1**

Mark   Isabelle   Claire

**2**

Spot   Fido   Blue

**3**

James   Sally   Robert

**1** (short) ? is the shortest.

**2** (small) ? is smaller than ? .

**3** (young) ? is younger than ? .

## Content Connection | Science

**12** Listen and read. How do mother alligators look after their young?

CONTENT WORDS

offspring    predator    protect    young (n.)

# Good Mothers

When this Surinam toad mother's babies were too young to swim on their own, their mother carried them on her back.

Mothers are very special people. They look after their children and want them to be healthy and safe. Animal mothers are the same. But the way they look after their offspring is sometimes a little different.

### Surinam Toad

Does your mum drive you to school or to your music lesson or sports practice? Can you imagine your mother carrying you and your brothers and sisters on her back all the time? That's what the Surinam toad, an animal from South America, does when she has babies. The Surinam toad mother carries as many as 100 babies on her back until they're old enough to swim by themselves.

### Orangutan

Does your mum help you tidy your room or make your bed? Maybe not any more. But that's exactly what the orangutan mother does for her offspring. Mother orangutans from Indonesia are the only animal mothers who make a new place for their babies to sleep in each night. They collect fresh leaves, twigs and branches and build their young a bed high in the trees.

### American Alligator

The world can be a scary and dangerous place when you are young, even if you are an alligator. That's why mother alligators keep their young in their mouth while they are moving over water or other dangerous places. In the past, when people saw this, they thought the mother was eating her own babies! She's actually protecting them from predators with her big, scary smile.

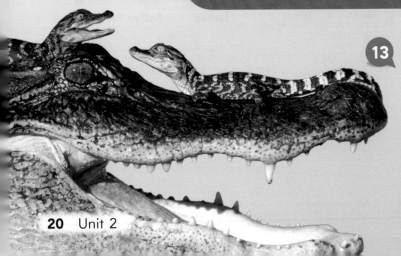

**13** Read 12 again and say true or false.

1 Surinam toad mothers can carry 100 babies on their backs.

2 Mother orangutans are the only animal mothers who build a new place for their babies to sleep in each night.

3 Alligator mothers sometimes eat their own babies.

**20** Unit 2

**1:30**
**14** Listen and read. Where do people
decorate trees with spider webs?

# Special Days for Families

Families around the world celebrate special days in special ways.
However, not all people celebrate the same special day in the same
way. Traditions for special days and holidays around the world are
as different as the countries and the people who celebrate them.
Some of these traditions may surprise you.

## Weddings

Getting married is one of the most important days in
the lives of many people around the world. In Germany,
the friends and family of the bride and groom gather a day
before the wedding. They break dishes, flower pots, bottles
and plates. Then the young couple has to clean it all up!
This tradition is called *polterabend*. Germans believe that it
brings good luck and strength to the new couple.

## Christmas

Holidays like Christmas are also different from place to place.
In Serbia, a lot of children celebrate the second Sunday before
Christmas as Mother's Day. On that day, children tie their
mother's feet to a chair and shout, "Mother's Day, Mother's Day!
What will you pay to get away?" The mother then gives presents
as payment to be freed. In Ukraine, many people decorate trees
with spider webs. They believe it brings good luck.

## Birthdays

In China, babies are one year old when they are born. After that,
all children celebrate their birthday on New Year's Day, even if it
is not their actual birthday. So New Year's Day is one big party!

**15** Read 14 again and match.

1 special          a have a good time
2 celebrate        b custom or habit
3 tradition        c not usual

**THINK BIG** Did you know about any of these traditions before?
Which ones surprised you? What family traditions from
other countries do you know about?

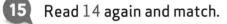
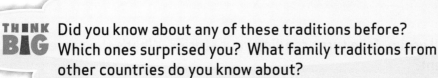

**16** Read Rosie's story.

## My Story
### by Rosie Harris

I was born in 2003. My family lived in Islington, London. When I was a year old, my family moved to St Albans. There were just three of us then: my mum, my dad and me. Two years later, we moved to Nottingham. We lived there until 2010. By then, I had two younger brothers. We needed a bigger house! So when I was seven, we moved to Peterborough. A few months ago, we went back to visit our old neighbourhood in Nottingham. I saw my old house. It looked even smaller than I remembered! Our family and our house are much bigger now!

**17** Copy and complete the chart with information from the story in 16.

| When? | What happened? |
|---|---|
| 2003 | I was born. We lived in Islington, London. |
| 2004 | |
| | We moved to Nottingham. |
| 2010 | |
| A few months ago | |

**18** Copy the chart into your notebook and complete it with information about your life so far. Then use it to write a story about you.

| When? | What happened? |
|---|---|
| | |
| | |
| | |

**19** Work in a small group. Take turns reading your stories. What's the same? What's different?

**20** What kind of family traditions do you have? Copy, read and ✔. Add one tradition of your own. Then ask a partner.

| Tradition | You | Your partner |
|---|---|---|
| **1** We visit our relatives on special holidays. | | |
| **2** We have a special meal on family birthdays. | | |
| **3** We have a family night at home every week. | | |
| **4** | | |

## PROJECT

**21** Make a page for a class book about family traditions.

**1** Include a drawing or a picture of your favourite family tradition.

**2** Write a short description about it.

**3** Share your page with the class.

My family has family night every Thursday.

Two years ago, we started a new family tradition. We have family night every Thursday night. We all make time to be together. Last week, we played a board game. I lost but it was fun.

**THINK BIG** What's your favourite family tradition? Why are family traditions important?

**22** Listen, read and repeat.

**1** g-e    ge      **2** g-i    gi      **3** g-y    gy

**23** Listen and blend the sounds.

**1** g-e-l          gel           **2** g-i-n-g-er      ginger

**3** g-y-m          gym           **4** g-y-p-s-y       gypsy

**5** g-i-r-a-ffe    giraffe       **6** g-e-m           gem

**24** Listen and chant.

A ginger giraffe
Worked out in a gym.
Quick! Get him some gel
For his hair!

**25** Complete the story. Make up the information.

**Aunt Isobel**

Aunt Isobel is a very interesting person. She was born in ? but her family moved to ? when she was ? years old. When she was in ? school, she had a collection of ? . It was probably the ? collection of ? in the world. People came from all over the world to see it. Now Aunt Isobel is ? years old and she lives in ? with ? .

**26** Take turns asking your classmates about their Aunt Isobel stories.

**1** Where was Aunt Isobel born?      **2** When did her family move?

**3** Where did they go?               **4** What kind of collection did Aunt Isobel have?

**5** Why was the collection special?  **6** How old is Aunt Isobel now?

**7** Where does she live now?         **8** Who does she live with?

**27** Complete the sentences. Use the correct form of the verb.

| be born | get married | graduate | move |
|---|---|---|---|

**1** My favourite aunt **?** from university two years ago.

**2** In 2007, his grandparents **?** to Bristol.

**3** When Celia's brother **?**, she was five years old.

**4** Our parents **?** 15 years ago.

**28** Complete the dialogue. Use the correct form of the words.

**Anna:** Who's that?

**Ben:** That's a picture of my grandma. She ¹**?** (graduate) from university this year.

**Anna:** That's amazing!

**Ben:** Yes, it is. She ²**?** (start) university when she was 57 years old. Years ago, when she ³**?** (be) young, some of her best friends ⁴**?** (go) to university but she was busy with her children. She didn't have time for university.

**Anna:** Was she the ⁵**?** (old) of all the graduates?

**Ben:** Actually, no. My grandma's friend Henry graduated, too. And he was even ⁶**?** (old) than my grandma. He was 72!

**I Can**

- talk about important life events that happened in the past.
- make comparisons.

# unit 3

# HELPING OTHERS

**1:34**

**1** Read about how children are helping others. Answer the questions with a partner. Then listen and check.

1 **Cupcakes for Cancer** Thirteen-year-old Blakely Colvin had a friend with leukemia, a kind of cancer. Blakely wanted to help her ill friend. What could she do? She decided to sell cupcakes after school. She sold her cupcakes for 50p each and, with the help of friends, they raised £1,800 in six weeks.

On average, how many cupcakes did Blakely and her friends bake every day?

2 **Creative Children for Charity** Chirag Vedullapalli wanted to do something to help others. He always loved to paint and draw. When he was nine years old, he decided he could sell his artwork and donate the money to a local children's hospital in Seattle, Washington, a big city on the west coast of the USA. Chirag's friends loved the idea, too. Chirag and ten of his friends each created one piece of art. They sold them for £10 each.

How much money did Chirag and his friends raise for the children's hospital?

3 **Biking for America** When Joseph Machado was 13 years old, he decided he could help children who are less fortunate and could do what he likes best, too – bike riding. He created Biking for America. Joseph rode his bike from California to Washington, DC, raising money along the way. Joseph rode his bike 120 kilometres a day for 39 days.

In total, how many kilometres did Joseph ride?

1:35

## 2 Read. Use the words from the boxes to complete the sentences. Then listen and check.

**A** The school choir is entering a big singing competition. The choir wants to buy new outfits for it. They need to raise money to buy them. Listen to their ideas:

art fair    cake sale    concert

| Fundraising | | |
|---|---|---|
| **1** We could have a/an ⚏. We could sell biscuits, pies and cakes. | **2** We could have a/an ⚏. Local artists could exhibit and sell their work. | **3** We could have a/an ⚏. We could perform songs and dances with a specific theme. |

**B** The choir has ideas for how to advertise their fundraising activities. Listen.

article    posters    video

| Advertising | | |
|---|---|---|
| **1** We're going to design colourful ⚏ and hang them up around school. | **2** I'm going to write a/an ⚏ about our activities for the school newspaper. | **3** I'm going to make a/an ⚏ of the choir performing and post it on the school website. |
|  |  |  |

## 3 Work with a partner. Ask and answer.

What could they do to raise money?

They could bake cakes and sell them.

What are they going to do to tell people about it?

They're going to make posters and hang them up around school.

**THINK BIG**  What else could they do to raise money?
How else could they advertise their fundraising activities?

**4** Listen and read. What did wburrington suggest?

www.dentonschool.org

# Denton School Blog

*On Wednesday 15ᵗʰ April at 1:37 p.m., Mr Thompson wrote…*

# FUNDRAISING TIME!

The Sports Department is asking pupils in years 7–10 to help out with this year's fundraising activities. We're going to use the money to help pay for new equipment, refreshments after matches and trips to matches at other schools.

If you've got any ideas for fundraising activities, please post them in the comments section below.

## COMMENTS

**cromano said**
We could sell chocolate bars. Who doesn't like chocolate?

**rmcnally said**
I like chocolate! Let's have a cake sale. We could sell chocolate cake, brownies and chocolate chip cookies. I'm getting hungry!

**wburrington said**
We could have a dance. My brother's class did that at his secondary school and they made a lot of money.

**jharmon said**
Yes, we could make something, like T-shirts with the name of our school on them. And then we could sell them on the school website.

**lscott said**
I've got a good idea! Why don't we have a 5 km fun run around the town? It could end on our school sports field and we could charge an entry fee and sell our school T-shirts, too.

**tjameson said**
At my junior school, we had a basketball shoot-out to raise money. Children had to pay to shoot ten balls and the person with the best score in each class got a prize. It was such fun!

( Login ) to add your comment below.

*On Monday 20th April at 9:02 a.m., Mr Thompson wrote...*

# FUNDRAISING UPDATE

Thanks for all the great ideas! The sports teachers and I discussed all the ideas you gave us and a few other ones. Here's the fundraising plan that we came up with for this year:

- Year 7: You're going to sell chocolate bars. We're going to order them from Charlie's Chocolates. They cost 50p each. Mr Campbell, the basketball teacher, is going to give you more information on Thursday.
- Year 8: You're going to sell water bottles with our school name and logo on them. The bottles cost £2.50 each. Miss Carpenter, the tennis teacher, is going to tell you more about it tomorrow after lunch.
- Year 9: You're going to have a dance and sell tickets to it. It's going to be in the school hall on Saturday night, 8th May. Ms Richards and Mr Benson, the football coaches, are going to meet you in the cafeteria next Tuesday before lunch to talk more about it.
- Year 10: You're going to have a cake sale. Mrs Fenton, the school nurse, is going to meet you this Friday, in the Year 10 common room, to give you more information.

We're all looking forward to this year's fundraising events. We know they're going to be a big success!

## READING COMPREHENSION

**5** Answer the questions with a partner.

1 What fundraising ideas did pupils post?

2 What is each year going to do to raise money?

**6** Find words in 4 with these meanings.

1 collecting money for a specific reason

2 items you need for a specific activity

3 drinks and snacks

THINK BIG Which fundraising idea do you think is the best? Why?
Write a comment with your own idea for a fundraising activity.

**7** Listen and read. What are the raffle winners going to get?

| | |
|---|---|
| **Vicky:** | Let's talk about how we're going to raise money for our class trip. Any ideas? |
| **Tanya:** | I've got an idea. We could all make something to sell. |
| **Vicky:** | Like what? |
| **Tanya:** | Well, we all like art. I like painting, you're good at sculpture and Susie likes taking photos… |
| **Caroline:** | So we could have an art exhibition here at the school. |
| **Tanya:** | Yes! |
| **Vicky:** | Wait a minute. Are people really going to buy our things? I'm not so sure. |
| **Caroline:** | Well, we could sell tickets to the exhibition. You know, raffle tickets. |
| **Vicky:** | Oh, I see. We sell raffle tickets and we pick the winners at the exhibition. The winners take home the art! |
| **Tanya:** | That sounds like a good idea! Let's tell the class. |

**8** Practise the dialogue in 7 with a partner.

**9** Listen and answer the questions.

**1** What could she do?

**2** What are they going to do?

**3** What's he going to do?

**4** What could she do?

| How **could** we raise money for our club? | We **could** have a car wash. |
|---|---|
| How much **could** they charge to wash one car? | They **could** charge £10 for a small car. For a bigger car, they **could** charge £15. |

**Tip:** Use *could* to express possibility or make suggestions.

**10** Complete the questions. Use how could or what could plus one of the words or phrases from the box.

> do to help    help people    make    raise money    tell people

1 **A:** 🝔 we 🝔 about the drama club?
   **B:** We could make posters.

2 **A:** 🝔 they 🝔 in their community?
   **B:** They could clean up the town park.

3 **A:** 🝔 she 🝔 us at the cake sale?
   **B:** She could put the icing on the cupcakes.

4 **A:** 🝔 they 🝔 for new equipment?
   **B:** They could have an art fair and sell their art work.

5 **A:** 🝔 I 🝔 for the art fair?
   **B:** You could make a collage.

| **Are** you **going to have** a concert? | Yes, we **are**. |
|---|---|
| How **are you going to tell** people about it? | We**'re going to make** posters. |

**Tip:** Use *is/am/are going to* to talk about events in the future.

**11** Complete the sentences with the correct form of be + going to.

**Lisa:** Our football team ¹🝔 have a cake sale next week.

**Paul:** Really? ²🝔 you 🝔 bake something?

**Lisa:** Uh… no. I'm not into baking.

**Paul:** So what ³🝔 you 🝔 do to help?

**Lisa:** I ⁴🝔 write an article for the school website.

**12** Listen and read. What makes a poster more attention grabbing?

> **CONTENT WORDS**
> advertisement  design  effective
> font  images  layout

# Creating an Effective Poster or Advert

What makes a poster or advertisement effective? A good poster or advert is one that gets your attention. It helps you focus on the important information.

To learn how to create an effective advert or poster, start by comparing the two posters on the right. Which one is more effective and why? Consider the following:

- font (the style of letters);
- font size (how big or small the letters are);
- font colour (colour of the letters);
- amount of text (too much text? not enough text? just right?);
- images (use of pictures); and
- layout (how the information is organised).

As you can see, the words are important but the design makes a big difference, too! The poster on the bottom has got less text but it includes colourful pictures. This makes the poster more attention grabbing.

Remember, only using big letters, a lot of colours and pictures aren't the only things you need to make a good poster. You have to have a good layout or design, as well. If your poster is too busy, your message might get lost!

**13** Read 12 again and match.

| | | | |
|---|---|---|---|
| 1 | images | a | how big or small the letters are |
| 2 | font | b | colour of the letters |
| 3 | layout | c | the style of letters |
| 4 | font colour | d | use of pictures |
| 5 | font size | e | how the information is organised |

CAKE SALE

Come to the gym today between 12–2 p.m. The school karate club is selling cupcakes to raise money for a field trip.

Enjoy a delicious cupcake for only 50p and support your school karate club!

CAKE SALE

Help the karate club raise money for a field trip. Enjoy a delicious cupcake today for only 50p!

Time:
12:00–2:00 p.m.

Place:
School gym

**14** Listen and read. What does Libby Mulligan do for charity?

# Doing What You Can

Many young people around the world raise money for charity groups. Charity groups help people (or animals!) in need. Read about what these young people are doing.

## A Song From the Heart
### Dublin, Ireland

Libby Mulligan loves to play the guitar and sing – and people love to listen to her. When she was 12 years old, she decided that she could play her guitar and sing at parties and weddings for money. No, Libby isn't a pop star yet. But she earns enough money to donate to a children's cancer charity in her community.

## Art for Animals
### Paris, France

Charles Lyon is a young artist who sells his art online to raise money for animal rescue. It all started when Charles wrote a letter to a local animal shelter asking what he could do to help stray cats and dogs in his neighbourhood. Then he came up with his website idea. Charles draws and sells pictures of animals on it. So far, he has sold more than 200 illustrations. He donates the money to local animal shelters and organisations that help find stray animals a new home.

## The Best Lessons
### Cape Town, South Africa

Tandi Jacobs and Stefan Burg wanted to help homeless children in their city. They decided to raise money by offering tutoring services. They used the money they earned to buy blankets, food and other supplies. More than 1,000 others have joined them, benefiting homeless children in other places around the country.

**15** Copy and complete.

1 ❓ plays the guitar and sings for a children's ❓ charity.

2 Charles Lyon ❓ of animals and then donates the money to a ❓ .

3 Tandi Jacobs and ❓ offer ❓ to raise money for ❓ children.

**THINK BIG** What international charity groups do you know about?
What kind of problem do you think you could help with? How?

**16** Read Michael's letter to his head teacher.

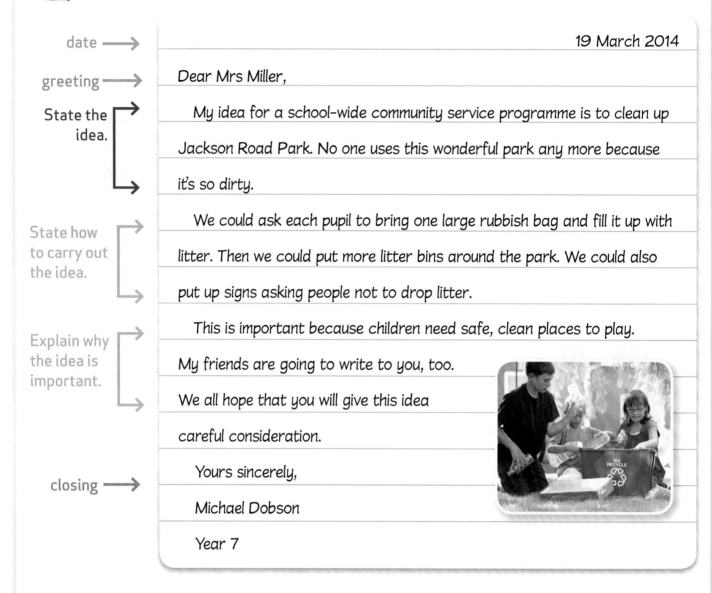

date →    19 March 2014

greeting → Dear Mrs Miller,

State the idea. → My idea for a school-wide community service programme is to clean up Jackson Road Park. No one uses this wonderful park any more because it's so dirty.

State how to carry out the idea. → We could ask each pupil to bring one large rubbish bag and fill it up with litter. Then we could put more litter bins around the park. We could also put up signs asking people not to drop litter.

Explain why the idea is important. → This is important because children need safe, clean places to play. My friends are going to write to you, too. We all hope that you will give this idea careful consideration.

closing → Yours sincerely,

Michael Dobson

Year 7

**17** What kind of school-wide community service programmes could you suggest to your head teacher? Discuss with a partner.

We could visit elderly people in a care home.

And we could visit ill children in a hospital.

**18** Choose one of your ideas and write a letter to your head teacher. Describe your idea and explain why it's important.

**19** Look at the names of the international charity groups. Match the name of the charity group to the description of the group.

**a** UNICEF

**b** Médecins Sans Frontières (Doctors Without Borders)

**c** Room to Read®

**d** WWF

**1** This international group sends doctors and nurses to help people in almost 70 countries around the world.

**2** This organisation builds libraries and gives books to children in many different countries across Asia and Africa.

**3** This group, part of the United Nations, works for the rights of children, including their rights to education, food, clean water and medical care.

**4** This conservation group works to protect the future of nature and animals. It's got more than five million supporters around the world.

## PROJECT

**20** Work in a small group. How could you raise money for a charity group? Write a fundraising plan. Then create an advert.

**Fundraising Plan**

Goal: *Raise £100 for animal shelter*
Activity: *School cake sale*
What: *Biscuits and cupcakes*
Where: *School playground*
When: *Next Monday lunchtime*
How: *Create an advert*

Idea for advert:
Your local animal shelter needs you.
Help homeless animals find a good home!
Enjoy a delicious cupcake after lunch for only 50p!
Time: 12 – 2 p.m. next Monday
Place: School playground

**THINK BIG** Which of the charities in 19 is the most interesting to you? Why? How could you help one of these groups?

# Listening and Speaking

 1:44

**21** Listen, read and repeat.

**1** l-k  lk        **2** m-b  mb

 1:45

**22** Listen and blend the sounds.

**1** w-a-lk        walk          **2** c-o-mb        comb

**3** l-a-mb        lamb          **4** t-a-lk        talk

**5** c-l-i-mb      climb         **6** ch-a-lk       chalk

 1:46

**23** Listen and chant.

> A lamb can walk
> But a lamb can't talk.
> A lamb is the colour of white chalk!

**24** Read the blog and comments. Follow the instructions. Discuss your choices with a partner. What else could you do?

www.dentonschool.org

# HELP BEAUTIFY OUR SCHOOL!

The art club needs your help! We're going to make our school beautiful this month. We've got to be resourceful and use what we've got on hand, such as basic art supplies. We haven't got money to spend. Look at these ideas people have suggested and choose the best ones. Remember, if it costs money, we probably can't do it.

**Comments**
- We could make a mural and hang it outside the office.
- We could replace the old office door.
- We could paint the old office door.
- We could organise the noticeboard and make it look more attractive.
- We could put some green plants in the hall.
- We could plant some flowers in front of the school.

**25** Read and complete.

**1** Your school band wants to raise money to buy some new drums.
What could you do? Write three ideas.

We could…

**2** Which idea is the best one? Why?

I think…

**3** Write three ways to tell people about your fundraising event. Use complete sentences.

We're going to…

**26** Read the poster. Then add what you could do to support the Walkathon.

**SUPPORT OUR WALKATHON!**

Walk from 1 to 10 km.
Or you could sponsor one of us.

Support Families in Need.
Every step counts!

### Sponsors

| | | |
|---|---|---|
| 1 | Mrs Madison | I'm going to give £2 for every kilometre my friend walks. |
| 2 | Jessie Kincaide | I'm going to walk 5 kilometres in the Walkathon. |
| 3 | your name | what you're going to do |

**I Can**

- talk about helping others and about fundraising activities.
- talk about possibilities.
- say what I'm going to do.

## How Well Do I Know It? Can I Use It?

**1** Think about it. Read and draw. Practise.

😊 I know this.　　😐 I need more practice.　　☹ I don't know this.

| | PAGES | | | |
|---|---|---|---|---|
| **Activities:** basketball team, drama club, school orchestra… | 3 | 😊 | 😐 | ☹ |
| **Life events:** was born, got married, graduated… | 15 | 😊 | 😐 | ☹ |
| **Fundraising activities:** have a cake sale, sell tickets, have an art fair… | 27 | 😊 | 😐 | ☹ |
| **Advertising:** make a poster, write an article, make a video… | 27 | 😊 | 😐 | ☹ |
| <u>How about</u> **joining** the school news bloggers?<br>I'm <u>interested in</u> **writing** articles.<br>She's <u>good at</u> **acting**. | 6–7 | 😊 | 😐 | ☹ |
| My family moved **when I was five**.<br>He graduated **six years ago**. | 18–19 | 😊 | 😐 | ☹ |
| How **could** we raise money for our school outing?<br>We **could** have a cake sale. | 30–31 | 😊 | 😐 | ☹ |
| What **are** you **going to do** for the cake sale?<br>I'**m going to bake** some biscuits. | 30–31 | 😊 | 😐 | ☹ |

## I Can Do It!

1:47

**2** **Get ready.**

**A** Complete the dialogue with the correct form of the verbs. Then listen and check.

**Mrs Rogers:** Everyone, I have news. Do you remember Mr Finnegan?

**Sandra:** Yes. He ¹ [?] (be) our music teacher when we ² [?] (be) in primary school.

**Jack:** Yes, I ³ [?] (have) my first violin lesson with him when I ⁴ [?] (be) six.

**Mrs Rogers:** Well, Mr Finnegan ⁵ [?] (retire) at the end of this school year. The head teacher ⁶ [?] (want) us to think of something we can do for him. Any ideas?

**Will:** I have one. Everyone could ⁷ [?] (write) a poem about Mr Finnegan. How about ⁸ [?] (put) them all together in a book?

**Sandra:** I don't know. I like ⁹ [?] (read) poems but I'm not good at ¹⁰ [?] (write) them.

**Jack:** I like ¹¹ [?] (write) poems. But I have another idea. I think we should ¹² [?] (take) a lot of photos around the school and we should ¹³ [?] (put) them on a big poster.

**Will:** Good idea! We could ¹⁴ [?] (write) funny notes next to the photos. Mr Finnegan would like that!

**B** Practise the dialogue in **A** with a partner.

**C** Ask and answer the questions with a partner.

1 What could the pupils write poems about?

2 What could the pupils take photos of?

3 Which idea do you think is better – the book of poems or the poster?

1
2
3
4
5
6
7
8
9

**3** Get set.

 **STEP 1** Cut out the cards on page 121 of your Activity Book.

 **STEP 2** Divide the cards into two sets: *A* cards in one set and *B* cards in another. Now you're ready to **Go!**

**4** Go!

A Look at the pictures. Make a dialogue for each picture using the *A* and *B* cards.

| Dialogue 1: Amanda and Kerry | Dialogue 2: Jacob and Thomas |

B Practise the two dialogues with a partner.

C Now make up your own dialogue. Choose one of these situations. Role play your dialogue in front of another pair.

### Situation 1:

| Pupil A | Pupil B |
| --- | --- |
| You're new at this school and you want to join a club. | You and your brother play sports. You're in several clubs at school, too. Give your new friend advice. |

### Situation 2:

| Pupil A | Pupil B |
| --- | --- |
| You're moving to another town soon. You're upset about moving. | You moved to this town when you were little. You remember how you felt when you moved. Give your friend advice. |

**5** Write about yourself in your notebook.

- Do you play sports at school or are you a member of a club?
- What kinds of things are you interested in doing in your free time?
- When did you start going to your current school?
- What school are you going to go to after this one?

All About Me    Date:_____

_____

_____

## How Well Do I Know It Now?

**6** Look at page 38 and your notebook. Draw again.

A  Use a different colour.

B  Read and think.

I can start the next unit.

I can ask my teacher for help and then start the next unit.

I can practise and then start the next unit.

**7** Rate this Checkpoint.

very easy

easy

hard

very hard

fun

OK

not fun

**2:01**

**1** Read. Guess the answer to each question. Then listen and check.

**1** What's an oniomaniac?

**a** Someone who shops too much.

**b** Someone who is afraid of shopping.

**c** Someone who eats too many onions.

**2** People in Banjarmasin, in Indonesia, get up early to buy their food. The market is open from 5:00 to 9:00 in the morning. The market sells fresh fruit, vegetables, fish, cakes and many other things. Why is this market more interesting than others?

**a** There are no shops.

**b** The sellers are all in boats!

**c** Both a and b.

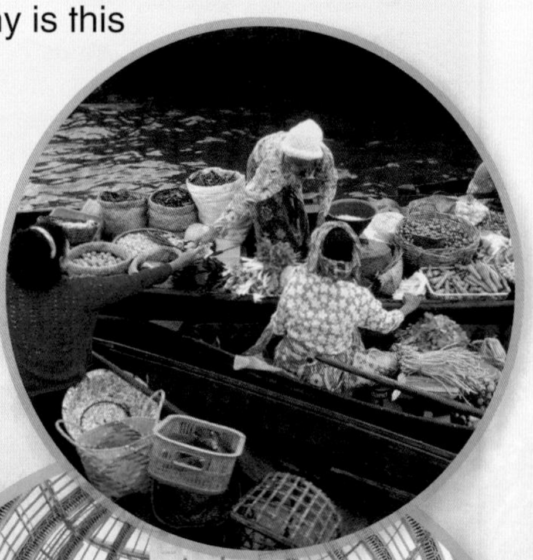

**3** The Dubai Mall in Dubai, United Arab Emirates, is the largest shopping centre in the world and has got the world's biggest sweet shop. It's also one of the most popular shopping centres in the world. How many people visited this shopping centre in 2011?

**a** 12 million

**b** 54 million

**c** 97 million

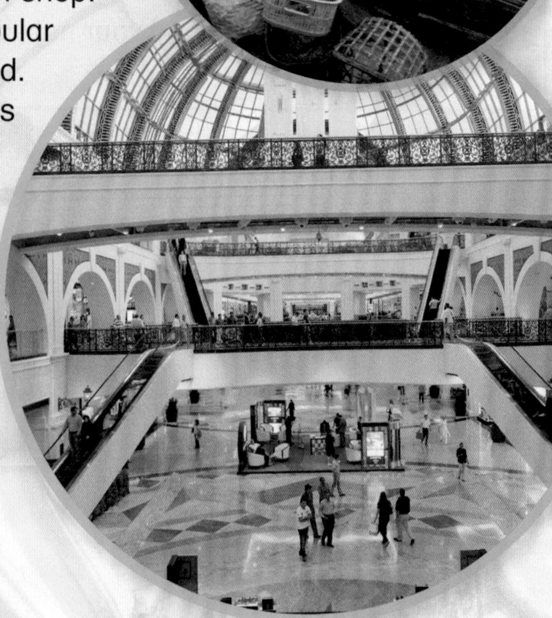

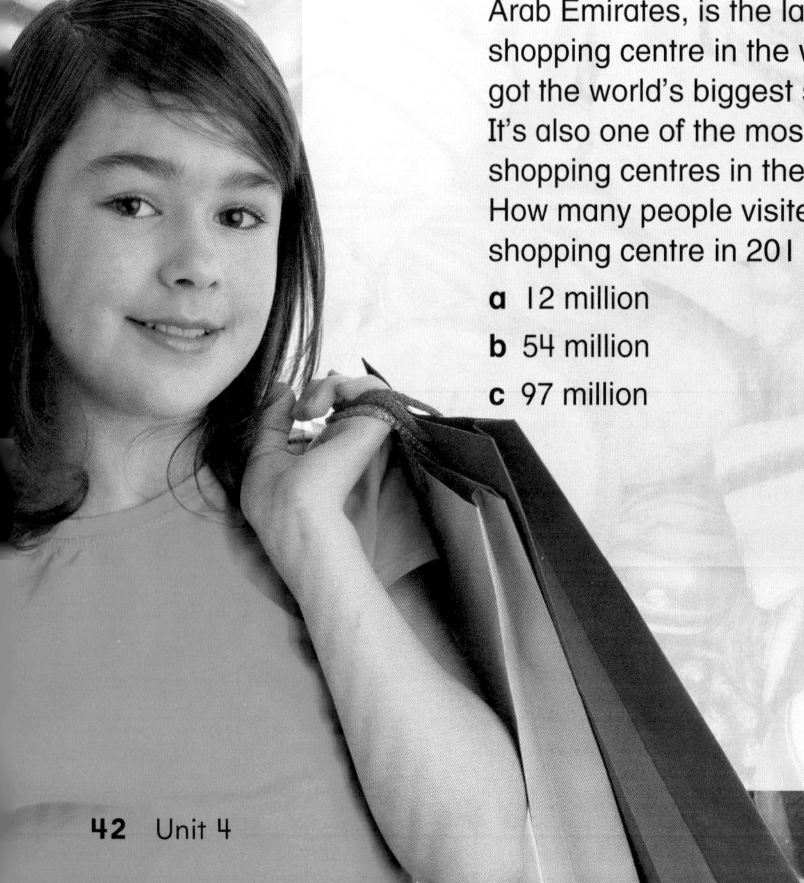

**2** Michelle and Dylan are talking about buying presents. What do they decide to buy? Listen and choose.

a beaded bracelet

a turquoise necklace

silver earrings

balloons

a picture frame

a bouquet of roses

2:03

**3** Listen again and take notes. Then choose the correct answers.

1 Michelle is going to buy her present at ❓ in the shopping centre.

 **a** a clothes shop   **b** a jewellery shop   **c** a department store

2 Dylan is going to buy his present at ❓.

 **a** a card shop   **b** a flower shop   **c** a craft fair

**4** Work with a partner. Ask and answer. Use your notes.

What does Michelle say about the silver earrings?

They're less expensive than the bracelet and they're beautiful.

**THINK BIG** Why do you think people give presents on Mother's Day?
How else can you celebrate Mother's Day?

**2:05**

**5** Listen and read. What's wrong with the earphones?

   www.reviewsbykids.com

▶ TV Shows

▶ Films

▶ Books

▶ Clothes

▼ Gadgets
- Digital Cameras
- Headphones
- mp3 Players
- Video Games

# REVIEWS BY KIDS
## THE WEBSITE BY AND FOR KIDS

Click on any category. Read a review or write a review. It's up to you!

**EAR PALS**     £10.99
Average Rating ★ ★ ☆ ☆ ☆

**REVIEWS**
★ ☆ ☆ ☆ ☆ **Never again!**
By Tamsin (Norwich)

My mum gave me a gift voucher for an online shop. I decided to use it to buy a pair of these headphones. They're called Ear Pals. I don't like them! The cords are too long and there's no case like the one they showed online. They aren't as good as they looked, that's for sure! Plus, the Ear Pals keep falling out of my ears. Maybe my ears are the wrong shape? Or maybe the wrong size? I don't know. These 'earphones' are definitely NOT my pals!     Read more reviews...

**CAMO-PHONES**     £20.95
Average Rating ★ ★ ★ ★ ☆

**REVIEWS**
★ ★ ★ ★ ★ **Fantastic!**
By muzik freak (Sheffield)

Good sound and great design. The camouflage design helps you hide when you're on a secret mission. They're a little expensive, it's true. But to me, they're worth the money. I used to buy less expensive headphones but they never lasted very long. Well, I learnt my lesson. Camo-Phones are the best.     Read more reviews...

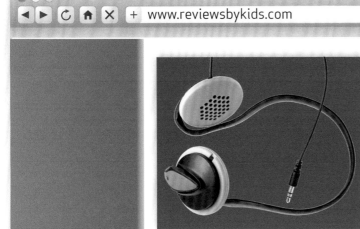

www.reviewsbykids.com

**BIG SOUND WRAP-AROUNDS**
£5.99
Average Rating ★ ★ ★ ☆ ☆

**REVIEWS**
★ ★ ★ ☆ ☆ **Good for the price**
By Danny

OK, maybe these aren't the best headphones in the world. They're definitely not as good as my old ones but at least they work. And they're the least expensive ones I know. The sound is just OK. Not good, not bad. But they're really cheap.

Read more reviews...

## READING COMPREHENSION

**6** Answer the questions with a partner.

1 Which headphones are the most expensive?
2 Which headphones are the least expensive?
3 Which headphones got the best review?
4 Which headphones got the worst review?

**THINK BIG** Which headphones do you think give the best value for money? Why? Which headphones would you buy? Why? Why do you think people read product reviews?

**2:07**
**7** Listen and read. Which game shop has got the cheapest prices?

**Karen:** What are you going to buy with your gift voucher?

**Josh:** A new game called Tunnel Island. I played it at Zack's house. It's really fun.

**Karen:** Great. So, where are you going to buy it?

**Josh:** That's what I'm trying to work out. I'm looking at prices online.

**Karen:** Good idea. Try looking at Game Time. No, wait. Look at Chester's. They're usually less expensive than Game Time.

**Josh:** Let me see… yes, you can find it at Chester's and it's only £25.00. I'm going to ask my mum to drive me there. Want to come?

**Karen:** OK.

**8** Practise the dialogue in 7 with a partner.

**2:08**
**9** Listen and find. Then choose a phrase from the box.

| a friend has got it | read an online review |
|---|---|
| saw it in a magazine | saw it on TV |

**a**

mp3
8GB
£70
FREE

**b**

SOLD OUT
4GB
£40
SALE
FREE

**c**

mp3
16GB
£100

**d**

mp3
8GB
£75

The blue shoes are **expensive**.

The red shoes are **more expensive than** the blue shoes.

The black shoes are **the most expensive** of all.

The red shoes are not **as expensive as** the black shoes.

The white shoes are **less expensive than** the blue shoes.

The white shoes are **the least expensive** of all.

**10** Complete the sentences. Use the adjective in brackets and more … than or the most.

1 *Summer's End* looks 💡 (interesting) *The Boys Are Back*.

2 *The Winning Game* is 💡 (interesting) book in the shop.

3 *Up the Stairs* is 💡 (exciting) of all the films here.

4 *Brain Power* is 💡 (exciting) *Mountain Rescue*.

5 *Great Escape* is 💡 (popular) *Find the Weasel*.

6 *Mind Bender* is 💡 (popular) video game of all.

7 *Super Invaders* is 💡 (expensive) *Spot the Alien*.

8 *Cowgirls* is 💡 (expensive) DVD here.

**11** Look at 10. Use as … as.

1 *The Boys Are Back* doesn't look 💡 *Summer's End*.

2 *Mountain Rescue* isn't 💡 *Brain Power*.

3 *Find the Weasel* isn't 💡 *Great Escape*.

4 *Spot the Alien* isn't 💡 *Super Invaders*.

| | |
|---|---|
| The price of those trainers is **too** high. | The price isn't low **enough**. |
| Those jeans are **too** baggy. | The jeans aren't tight **enough**. |

**12** Make sentences in your notebook. Use too or enough and a word from each box.

| board game | coat | curry | sandals |

| comfortable | expensive | spicy | warm |

2:10

**13** Listen and read. When were the first coins used?

**CONTENT WORDS**

bronze   coins   grain   livestock   metal   paper money   shells   trade

# MONEY, MONEY, MONEY!

Most people today use coins, paper money or credit cards to buy things. However, shopping wasn't always as easy as that.

About 10,000 years ago, people farmed and grew the food they needed. They raised livestock, like cows and goats, and grew grain, like rice and wheat. During that time, people used livestock and grain as money in many different parts of the world. Imagine paying for your new video game with a couple of goats!

Over the years, things changed and about 3,000 years ago, people started to use other things as money. Shells from the sea, such as the *cowrie shell*, were traded as money in places like China, Thailand, India and some countries in Africa.

It wasn't until about 2,000 years ago when the first coins appeared. China, Greece and India were probably the first places to use metal coins. Most coins were made of expensive metals like bronze, silver or gold.

But carrying around a lot of heavy coins wasn't much fun. That's probably why paper money started to be used almost 1,000 years ago.

**14** Look at 13. Copy and complete.

| When? | Where? | What was used as money? |
|---|---|---|
| **1** 10,000 years ago – many different parts of the world – ❓ | **2** ❓ – China, Thailand and India – cowrie shells | **3** 2,000 years ago – China, Greece and India – ❓ |

**THINK BIG** How do you think people decided on what to use as money?
How do you think people will pay for things in the future?

**2:17**

**15** Listen and read. What can you buy at Electric Town?

# SHOP till you DROP

Do you love to shop? Find out about some of the world's most exciting shopping adventures!

### The Thai Experience - Chatuchak Market, Bangkok

The Chatuchak Weekend Market in Bangkok, Thailand is one of the biggest markets in the world and one of the most famous. The market is huge – more than 35 acres in all. It's got more than 15,000 sellers and more than 200,000 people visit every weekend. Here you can find everything from a designer pair of jeans to a cute little puppy! Just remember, Chatuchak is really big so don't get lost!

### Excitement in Electric Town, Tokyo

In Tokyo, Japan, one of the most popular places for young people is called Akihabara. Akihabara is not a shop. It's a neighbourhood that is known as 'Electric Town'. Young people come from all over the world to buy the latest electronics, video games, animation, computers and more.

### Finding Everything in Camden Market

It's a rainy morning and you are in London. The sky is grey and you want something interesting to do. Why not head to Camden Market? Every day in Camden Market artists and vendors sell their goods in this (mostly) indoor market. With fine arts, traditional crafts, jewellery, clothes, great food and music, there's something here for everyone!

**16** Read 15 again and answer the questions.

1 Where can you buy a puppy?
2 What can you buy in Camden Market?
3 What is Akihabara?

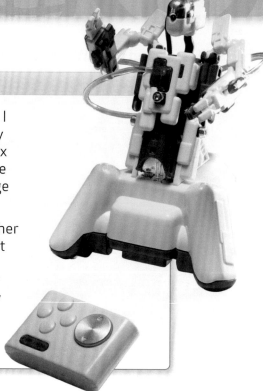

**17** Read the product review.

> I saved my pocket money for a long time. Then finally, I decided what I wanted to buy. My dad and I bought my remote-controlled robot at Talford's. I brought the box home and opened it. I read the instructions. I put in the batteries. Then I turned the robot on. It made a strange sound and fell over! My new robot didn't work.
>
> So we took it back to the shop and they gave me another robot. I took that one home and it worked fine. I wasn't happy about the first robot but I'm very happy now. This robot is really great. It's more expensive than my other gadgets but it was worth the money. I definitely recommend it.
>
> My Rating ★ ★ ★ ☆

**18** Look at the word web. Ask and answer with a partner. Find the answers in 17.

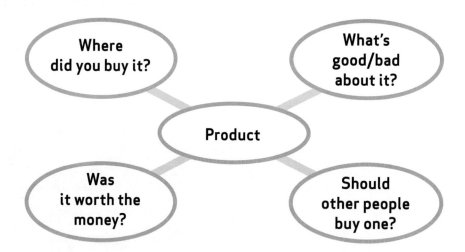

**19** Choose your own product. Copy the word web in 18 into your notebook. In each circle, write answers to the questions. Then use the word web to write your own product review.

**20** Share your product reviews with the class. How many good reviews were there? How many bad reviews were there?

**21** What do you do with your money? Copy, read and ✔. Then ask a partner.

| | always | usually | sometimes | never |
|---|---|---|---|---|
| **1** I spend all my money straight away on things I want. | | | | |
| **2** I like to save my money to buy the things I need. | | | | |
| **3** I use my money to buy presents for other people. | | | | |
| **4** I put my money in a bank. Then I forget about it. | | | | |

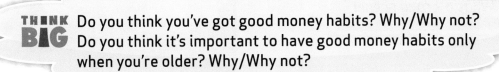

**THINK BIG** Do you think you've got good money habits? Why/Why not?
Do you think it's important to have good money habits only when you're older? Why/Why not?

**PROJECT**

**22** Design a shopping bag for a shop that helps you spend your money wisely. Be sure to give your shop a name!

**23** Work in small groups. Talk about your shopping bags.

Spend Smart Shop
Use our bags and SAVE 10p
We have the lowest prices. If you find something less expensive at another shop, We'll match the price! TO SAVE use our Smart card to earn a FREE MEAL!

# Listening and Speaking

2:12

**24** Listen, read and repeat.

1 s-c    sc         2 h-o    ho

2:13

**25** Listen and blend the sounds.

| | | | | |
|---|---|---|---|---|
| **1** m-u-sc-le | muscle | **2** e-c-ho | echo |
| **3** ho-n-e-s-t | honest | **4** sc-ie-n-ce | science |
| **5** g-ho-s-t | ghost | **6** sc-e-ne | scene |

2:14

**26** Listen and chant.

An honest ghost
Made an echo
In our science class.
Wow! What a crazy scene!

**27** What can you buy or see at a shopping centre? Work in pairs. Play More or Less.

First, complete the sentences with your own answers.

1 ❓ are delicious.

2 ❓ are expensive.

3 ❓ is an interesting book.

4 ❓ is an exciting film.

5 ❓ is an amazing shop.

6 ❓ is a useful gadget.

Hot dogs are
delicious.

Burgers are more
delicious than hot dogs.

**28** Look, copy and complete. Use more or less.

1 The bike is ❓ expensive than the skateboard.

2 The calculator is ❓ expensive than the game.

3 The jeans are ❓ expensive than the jacket.

4 The watch is ❓ expensive than the necklace.

**29** Discuss. What's the most expensive thing at the jumble sale? What's the least expensive thing at the jumble sale?

**I Can**

• **talk about shopping.**

• **make comparisons.**

# unit 5

# HOLIDAY TIME

**2:15**

**1** Read and complete these fun facts about holidays. Use words from the box. Then listen and check.

kayak   mobile phones   mosquitoes   sunburnt

### 1 Lost and Found

In 2011, more people lost their ❓ than their sunglasses while they were travelling!

### 2 Ouch!

Every year, ❓ make 700 million people ill!

### 3 Cover up!

Be careful! You can get ❓ on a cloudy day if you don't wear sunscreen!

### 4 Why not fly?

In 2010, a British woman took the longest ❓ trip that anyone has ever taken – more than 3,200 kilometres!

**2** Match. Then listen and check.

**1** insect repellent    **2** a helmet    **3** a warm jacket

**4** an anorak    **5** a life jacket    **6** water bottle

**7** a map    **8** sunscreen    **9** sunglasses

**a**

**b**

**c**

**d**

**e**

**f**

**g**

**h**

**i**

**3** Look at the words in the word box. Choose three activities you like. Why do you like them?

| Activity | Reason |
|---|---|
|  |  |
|  |  |
|  |  |

biking
camping
hiking
horse riding
kayaking
rafting
skiing
swimming

**4** Work with a partner.
Ask and answer.

What happened when she was hiking?

She got thirsty.

**THINK BIG** What are the five most important things you should take with you when hiking?

2:17

**5** Listen and read. Why did Jenny enjoy the weekend?

# The BEST WEEKEND EVER

## by Alison Green

Jenny and her mother were getting ready for a camping trip. Mum was packing their food when Jenny walked into the kitchen.

"Can't we stay at home?" Jenny asked. "I really don't want to go camping," she said.

"But camping is so much fun!" said Mum.

"Sleeping in a tent?" said Jenny. "No TV? That's fun?"

"Yes, it is. We can go hiking! We can make a fire! We can cook sausages outside!" said Mum.

Jenny and her mother arrived at the campsite. They took everything out of the car. Jenny looked up at the sky.

"It's getting cloudy," said Jenny. Suddenly they heard thunder. KABOOM!

"Oh, no!" said Mum. "Let's set up the tent!"

Jenny and Mum were setting up the tent when it started to rain.

"Quick! Get inside the tent!" said Mum.

Jenny waited inside the tent. In a few minutes, Mum came inside, too. Her hair was wet. Her clothes were wet. Her shoes were wet. Everything was wet.

Jenny played her video game while her mother made jam sandwiches. They ate them inside the tent.

It rained all night. And it rained the next day. It rained the whole weekend! Jenny and her mum sat inside. They couldn't go hiking. They couldn't make a fire. They couldn't cook any sausages outside.

After two days of rain, Jenny's mother said, "Time to go home. Please help me take down the tent, Jenny," she said. "Then wait in the car." Jenny waited inside the car with her video game.

While Jenny's mother was packing everything into the car, it stopped raining. Then the sun came out. "Now it's sunny," Mum said. She got into the car and started driving home.

Mum said, "You were right, Jenny. That wasn't much fun."

"What? I had a great time, Mum!" said Jenny. "I ate jam sandwiches all weekend and I reached Level 12 on my video game. It was the best weekend ever!"

## READING COMPREHENSION

**6** Choose the correct answers.

**1** When Jenny was looking at the sky, what did she hear?
  **a** She heard thunder.
  **b** She heard rain.

**2** Why didn't Jenny and her mum go hiking?
  **a** Because it rained all weekend.
  **b** Because Jenny was playing her video game.

**3** What did Jenny and her mum eat?
  **a** They ate sausages.
  **b** They ate jam sandwiches.

**4** What was Jenny doing while her mum was packing the car to go home?
  **a** She was making a fire.
  **b** She was waiting in the car.

**5** When did it stop raining?
  **a** While Jenny's mum was packing everything into the car.
  **b** While they were driving home.

**6** What did Jenny think about the camping trip?
  **a** She hated it.
  **b** She loved it.

**THINK BIG** Do you think Jenny would like to go camping again? Why/Why not?
Do you like camping? Why/Why not?

# Language in Action

**7** 2:19   Listen and read. Why was this Daniel's best holiday ever?

**Louise:** Hi, Uncle Daniel. It's Louise. How was your holiday?

**Daniel:** Hi, Louise. It was great. It was the best holiday ever!

**Louise:** Oh, really? What did you do?

**Daniel:** Well, the first day, I went to the beach. While I was lying on the sand, I fell asleep and woke up with terrible sunburn.

**Louise:** Oh, no. Really?

**Daniel:** Yes, so the next day I went hiking in the forest. While I was hiking, I got dozens of mosquito bites.

**Louise:** Oh, no!

**Daniel:** Yes. And so the next day I went horse riding. While I was riding, the horse got scared and jumped. I fell off the horse and broke my leg.

**Louise:** Oh, that's awful! But Uncle Daniel, I'm confused. So why was this the best holiday ever?

**Daniel:** The doctor says I need to stay at home for a week. I can finally rest and relax!

**8** Practise the dialogue in 7 with a partner.

**9** 2:20   What happened on Gina's holiday? Listen and match. Then complete the sentences. Use the correct form of the verb.

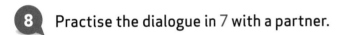

eat    read    shop    try to sleep

**1** She ? when it happened.     **2** She ? when it happened.

**3** She ? when it happened.     **4** She ? when it happened.

| What **was** he **doing** when he got hurt? | He **was riding** a horse when he got hurt. |
| What happened while they **were hiking**? | They got lost while they **were hiking**. |

**10** Complete the sentences with the correct form of the verb in brackets.

1 Samuel ❓ when he got thirsty. (hike)

2 They were kayaking when it ❓ to thunder. (start)

3 They ❓ for the bus when it started to rain. (wait)

4 I ❓ my bracelet while I was swimming. (lose)

5 Alicia broke her leg while she ❓ . (ski)

6 He ❓ when he fell in the road. (skateboard)

7 We ❓ life jackets when we fell in the sea. (wear)

8 Jeremy ❓ the sausages while he was cooking dinner. (burn)

| **Was** he **riding his bike** when it started to rain? | Yes, he **was**./No, he **wasn't**. |
| **Were** you **swimming** when you got sunburnt? | Yes, I **was**./No, I **wasn't**. |

**11** Make questions.

1 (when/Tim/Was/hiking) ❓ his sunglasses broke?

2 (Billy and Lisa/biking/Were/when) ❓ they suddenly heard thunder?

3 (shopping/Dan/when/Was) ❓ he lost his mobile phone?

4 (when/you/Were/horse riding) ❓ you got stung by the bee?

5 (Were/the hotel/his parents/when/checking into) ❓ the lights went out?

6 (Sarah/camping/when/Was) ❓ she broke her arm?

**2:22**

**12** Listen and read. What happened to the backpack?

---

**CONTENT WORDS**

addition    customer    item    multiplication    realise    total

---

You work in a shop at Greenfell Mountain National Park and sell these items:

| sunscreen £6.99 | disposable camera £9.99 | crisps £1.09 |
|---|---|---|
| insect repellent £5.49 | map of the park £2.50 | apple 75p |
| sunglasses £12.99 | bottle of water £1.25 | postcards 90p |

Use addition and multiplication to find the totals for these customers and write them in your notebook:

**1** "Hello. This is my first time hiking and I need some suggestions for what to get. Oh, never mind. I see you've put up a list of suggestions. Perfect! Let's see… insect repellent, sunscreen, two bottles of water and a map. I think that's all. I needn't buy anything else. Wait. I'll have an apple and a bag of crisps, too. How much is it?"

**2** "Hi. I'm so glad this shop is here. While we were driving here, I realised I didn't have any insect repellent. Can I get three bottles of that, please? Oh, and I forgot to bring a snack for my Year 5 pupils. So I need 15 apples. How much is that?"

**3** "Oh, hi. Listen. Guess what happened to me? I was out hiking this morning when I saw this beautiful flower. I tried to take a picture of it. But while I was opening my backpack, I heard an animal sound and dropped it. My backpack fell down the side of the mountain! Grr! One disposable camera, please. I'm going to try again. Oh, and I need to buy a bottle of water and a pair of sunglasses, too. Everything was in that bag! So, how much is it altogether?"

**13** Read 12 again and say true or false.

**1** Customers can get advice about what they need.

**2** The teacher needs a bottle of insect repellent for each child in his class.

**3** The woman dropped her backpack when she heard a noise.

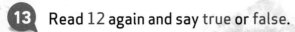

> **THINK BIG** Who spent the most money? Who spent the least money? What would you buy at the national park with £25? Why?

**14** Listen and read. Where can you stay in an igloo?

# UNIQUE
## Holiday Destinations

Every year, millions of people around the world go on holiday. Some visit their families who live far away. Some visit national parks and others just lie on the beach. Would you like to try something different for your next holiday? Here are a few suggestions.

Try looking at some bad art! The Museum of Bad Art, near Boston, Massachusetts, USA, has got more than 600 pieces of the world's worst art. But is the art really that bad?

Put on your warm coat (a *very* warm coat) and head over to Ilulissat, Greenland. From there you can go on an expedition into frozen lands where Arctic foxes, polar bears and other amazing animals live. When else will you have the chance to stay overnight in an igloo?

The Alnwick Garden in Northumberland, UK, has got beautiful flowers and plants but remember, it's known as the Poison Garden for a good reason! Pay close attention to the signs that say, "Do not touch the plants. Do not even smell them!" But don't be afraid. Tours of the garden will tell you everything you need to know about these dangerous but fascinating plants.

The airport on St Maarten, an island in the Caribbean, is close to the beach. Too close! Every year, thousands of people stand on the beach and wait for planes. The planes fly right over their heads. It's the closest that you and a plane will ever get unless you're on one!

The Museum of Bad Art

Igloo Village

The Alnwick Garden

Maho Beach

**15** Read 14 again and answer the questions.

1 How many pieces of the world's worst art can you see at The Museum of Bad Art?

2 Why is the Alnwick Garden also known as the Poison Garden?

3 Where can you get very close to a plane?

**16** Read Helen's postcard.

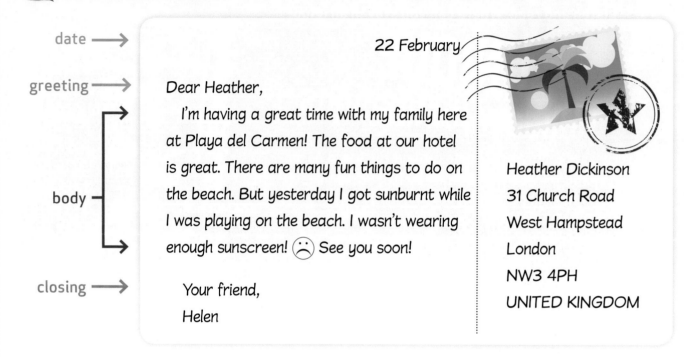

date →

22 February

greeting →

Dear Heather,

body →

    I'm having a great time with my family here at Playa del Carmen! The food at our hotel is great. There are many fun things to do on the beach. But yesterday I got sunburnt while I was playing on the beach. I wasn't wearing enough sunscreen! ☹ See you soon!

closing →

    Your friend,
    Helen

Heather Dickinson
31 Church Road
West Hampstead
London
NW3 4PH
UNITED KINGDOM

**17** Read the Writing Steps and write a postcard to a friend about your holiday.

## Writing Steps

**1** Think of a holiday place.

**2** Write a date and greeting.

**3** Write about where you are.

**4** Write about why you like it or don't like it.

**5** Write about a problem on your holiday.

**6** Write a final sentence.

**7** Write a closing and sign the postcard.

**8** Write an address.

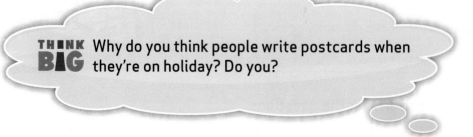

THINK BIG Why do you think people write postcards when they're on holiday? Do you?

**18** Work in pairs and discuss. Where do you like to go on holiday? Copy the chart into your notebook and list the kinds of places. Then take turns writing safety tips.

| Holiday Place | Pupil 1 Tip | Pupil 2 Tip |
|---|---|---|
| The beach | Don't swim straight after eating. | |
| The mountains | | |
| | | |
| | | |

## PROJECT

**19** Work with another pair. In your group, make a poster about one of your holiday places. Include your safety tips. Add pictures. Share your poster with the class.

**SAFETY TIPS**
for the **Amusement Park**

**1** Always wear sunscreen.

**2** Take along a water bottle. Drink water often.

**3** Know how to contact your parents.

**4** Decide on a time and place to meet.

**5** Hold onto your camera and other important items.

**6** Don't talk to strangers.

**2:24**

**20** Listen, read and repeat.

1 c-l    cl        2 t-w    tw

**2:25**

**21** Listen and blend the sounds.

| 1 | cl-ow-n | clown | 2 | tw-i-n | twin |
|---|---------|-------|---|--------|------|
| 3 | tw-i-s-t | twist | 4 | cl-o-ck | clock |
| 5 | tw-e-l-ve | twelve | 6 | cl-a-p | clap |

**2:26**

**22** Listen and chant.

> It's twelve o'clock. Time to twist.
> It's twelve o'clock. Time to clap.
> Twist, twist, twist! Clap, clap, clap!

**23** Play the Crazy Holiday Game! First, choose a word or phrase in each numbered row. Then copy the dialogue and complete it with your choices. Take turns practising the dialogue with different partners.

| 1 | far away | clean | romantic | dirty |
|---|----------|-------|----------|-------|
| 2 | skiing | drawing | cycling | bird-watching |
| 3 | best | worst | most boring | most exciting |
| 4 | delicious | old | expensive | spicy |
| 5 | Antarctica | the Himalayas | Easter Island | the Sahara Desert |
| 6 | get hot | rain | snow | get windy |

| **Ted:** | I just got back from holiday. |
|----------|-------------------------------|
| **Joanna:** | Really? How was it? |
| **Ted:** | It was the ³ 🔖 holiday ever. |
| **Joanna:** | Wow. Where did you go? |
| **Ted:** | I went to ⁵ 🔖. |
| **Joanna:** | That sounds great. |
| **Ted:** | Yes. The food was ⁴ 🔖 and the hotel was ¹ 🔖. |
| **Joanna:** | Wow. That sounds really nice. |
| **Ted:** | Uh-huh. But I had some problems, too. While I was ² 🔖, it started to ⁶ 🔖. |
| **Joanna:** | Oh, no! That's terrible. |
| **Ted:** | Yes, but it turned out OK. I'm happy to be home now. |
| **Joanna:** | Great. I can't wait to see your holiday photos! |

**24** Copy and complete the chart. Some words can be used more than once.

> a helmet     an anorak        a life jacket    a map
> a water bottle   insect repellent   sunscreen    walking shoes

What should you take along when you go…

| kayaking? | hiking? | biking? |
|---|---|---|
|  |  |  |

**25** Complete the email.

> hiking    mosquito bites    sunburnt    swimming

Hi, Grandma!

We're all having a great time at the beach. Except for Dad. He isn't having a great time. While he was ¹ 🔲 yesterday, he got ² 🔲. He forgot his sunscreen! And Mum isn't having a great time either. While she was ³ 🔲 in the woods, she got a lot of ⁴ 🔲. She forgot her insect repellent. But now we're in the hotel. We're going to order pizza! See you soon.

Love,
Paul

**26** Match the questions and answers.

1 What were you doing when it started to rain?

2 Were you wearing sunscreen when the sun came out?

3 What happened while Ed was riding the horse?

4 Did Sandra have insect repellent on when the mosquitoes bit her?

a No, she didn't.

b I was hiking in the woods.

c He fell off!

d Yes, we were.

**I Can**

• talk about holiday problems.

• talk about what was going on when something happened.

# THE FUTURE!

2:27

**1** Read about these inventions. Are they real or not real? Then listen and check.

### I KEYBOARD JEANS

Keyboard jeans are the latest fashion trend. These jeans come with built-in speakers, a wireless mouse and a keyboard built into the legs of the trousers. This gives new meaning to the term 'laptop' computer!

### 2 SPRAY-ON BATTERY

The battery in a mobile device can take up almost half of the space in your mobile phone, smartphone or tablet. But now there's a spray-on battery! This battery will be 'painted' onto your mobile device, taking up no room at all.

### 3 COMPUTER EYEGLASSES

With these computer glasses, you'll be able to do everything you do on a normal computer. There's one big difference: You won't have to carry anything! The lenses are a see-through computer monitor.

### 4 PET TRAINING APP

Tired of trying to stop your dog from barking in the house? Well, now there's an app for that! This new app for smartphones will stop your dog barking at the touch of a button. It uses special sounds that only dogs understand. You just have to make sure your dog is listening!

**2** Listen and find. Which electronic device is the girl talking about? Then match with the correct words and phrases from the box.

a

b

c

d

laptop computer
mp3 player
smartphone
tablet

**3** Listen again. Will we have these devices ten years from now? Copy and make two lists. Can you add any of your own ideas?

| In ten years, we will still have them. | In ten years, we probably won't have them. |
|---|---|
|  |  |

**4** Work in small groups. Ask and answer.

Will people still use mobile phones ten years from now?

Yes, they will. People will always use mobile phones.

No, they won't. People will find easier ways to communicate.

**THINK BIG** In ten years' time, what will be the biggest changes at school?
In ten years' time, what will be the biggest changes at home?

2:30

5 Listen and read. What happened to the flowers on Rozul?

# The Visitor

by Bryan Valverde

When the spaceship landed, the boy was hiding behind the trees. It was a beautiful clear morning. The sun was shining. The birds were singing. The boy just watched the spaceship and waited.

While the boy was watching and waiting, a tall creature suddenly came out of the spaceship. The creature was wearing a silver suit and a large helmet. He started collecting flowers. One by one, he scanned each flower with some kind of camera. Then he typed some information about the flower onto a tablet. When he was finished, he put the flower into a large box.

The creature thought he saw something move and asked, "Is anybody there?" The boy didn't answer.

The creature looked over his shoulder and saw the boy hiding behind the trees. "Oh, there is someone. Hello!" the creature said, "It's all right. You can come closer."

"What are you doing?" the boy asked.

"I'm collecting samples… of flowers," the creature replied.

"Flowers? For what?" asked the boy.

"I'm going to take them back to my planet," said the creature.

"Haven't you got any flowers on your planet?" asked the boy.

The creature sighed. "No, our planet dried up a long time ago. We created too much pollution, we cut down too many trees and now it's like a desert. There's almost no water any more. All of the flowers and trees that lived on our planet are gone."

"That's terrible," said the boy. "Is anyone doing anything about it?"

"Yes. That's why we're collecting samples of life from other planets. Our scientists are working very hard to create water. We use these samples to learn about water. I believe someday, water will return to our planet."

"Wow," the boy said. "What's the name of your planet?"

"It's called Rozul," the creature said. "Long ago, it was very beautiful. If we work hard, someday Rozul will be beautiful again." And then the creature returned to his ship. The boy waved goodbye as the spaceship slowly went up into the air and disappeared.

## READING COMPREHENSION

**6** Read and say true or false.

1 The boy lives on Rozul.

2 The creature finds out that someone is hiding.

3 There's water on the boy's planet.

4 The creature is collecting samples of flowers.

5 Scientists on the creature's planet are trying to create plants.

**THINK BIG** Do you think the Earth will always have enough water? Why/Why not? What one thing can everyone do to save water? What can you do to save water on our planet? Name at least two things.

**2:32**

**7** Listen and read. How will Ellie get to school today?

**Dad:** Listen to this. Somebody has invented a flying suit. Can you believe it?

**Ellie:** Yes, I've heard about it. I want one!

**Dad:** Start saving your money. This one costs £75,000!

**Ellie:** Wow. That is expensive! But it won't be expensive in the future. Someday, everybody will have one.

**Dad:** You're probably right.

**Ellie:** We'll simply put on flying suits and fly wherever we want. No more planes or airports!

**Dad:** OK. But today – no flying suits for you! You're going to go on the bus. And you'd better hurry up!

**8** Practise the dialogue in 7 with a partner.

**2:33**

**9** Listen and match. Then write. Use a word or phrase from the box.

> computer navigation system     smartphone
> tablet    video messaging

| **1** We'll use ❓ to talk to our friends. | **2** We'll use our ❓ to pay for things. | **3** We'll use a ❓ to attend school virtually. | **4** We'll use a ❓ to tell our cars where we want to go. |
|---|---|---|---|

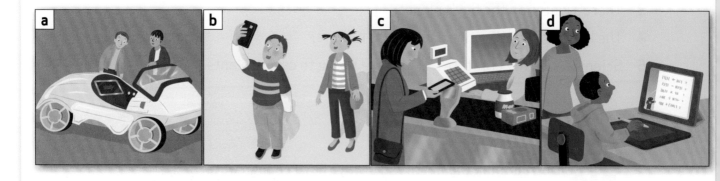

| Do you think we**'ll have** cars 100 years from now? | Yes, we **will**. But cars **won't have** drivers! They**'ll use** computers. |
| | No, we **won't**. We**'ll have** spaceships. |

**10** Make predictions about the future. Use won't and will.

1 write letters/send emails

2 buy things in shops/shop online

3 use telephones/use video chatting

4 attend school/use virtual classrooms

5 play with dolls/play with robots

| Who will use video messaging in the future? | **Anyone** with a computer and internet access will use video messaging. |
| Who will send letters to communicate with friends in the future? | **No one/Nobody** will send letters to communicate with friends. |
| | **Everyone/Everybody** will use email. |
| | Well, **someone** might write a letter! |

**11** Make predictions about the future. Use no one, someone or everyone with will or might.

1 Who will use tablets instead of desktop computers?

2 Who will use a smartphone 100 years from now?

3 Who will use driverless cars?

4 Who will watch DVDs?

5 Who will go to virtual shopping centres?

**2:36**

**12** Listen and read. What is the 'big screen'?

> **CONTENT WORDS**
> assistive   gestures   procedures   robotic   socially   surgical

# THE ROBOTS AROUND US

What is the first thing that comes to mind when you think about robots? Maybe *Wall-E*, the Disney robot designed to collect rubbish, who accidentally ends up saving the planet? Or maybe the lovable robots R2D2 and C3PO from the *Star Wars* films? Those kinds of robots are still only possible on the big screen.

Most robots today are made to help do work that nobody wants to do or work nobody can do. There are more than a million robots doing all kinds of work for us already. For example, the Mars rover *Sojourner* and the underwater robot *Caribou* help us learn about places that are too difficult or dangerous for anyone to go.

## SNAKEBOTS

One of the most amazing robots today is called a *snakebot*. This robotic arm is long and thin and can move almost like a real snake. It can move forward and sideways and even upwards. These snakebots can go where no one else can. That means they might be able to help find someone trapped in a building after an earthquake or a fire. Some people think snakebots will be used in surgical procedures.

## MAN'S BEST FRIEND?

*Socially Assistive Robots* can talk, move around and even make common gestures with their hands. The makers of these robots hope that one day they'll help people with special problems. One good thing about a robot is that it never gets tired or angry. So it will always be there to help. Now that really is a good friend!

**13** Read 12 again and match.

| | | | |
|---|---|---|---|
| 1 | assistive | a | movements |
| 2 | gestures | b | medical |
| 3 | procedures | c | helpful |
| 4 | surgical | d | processes |

2:37

**14** Listen and read. Why is Kallawaya known as a secret language?

# ENDANGERED LANGUAGES

Just like animals and plants, languages can become extinct over time. About every 14 days, one of the 7,000 languages in the world is no longer spoken and dies.

By the year 2100, more than half of the languages spoken in the world today will be extinct.

## A SECRET LANGUAGE

There are more than 30 languages spoken in Bolivia today. One language, Kallawaya, is known as a *secret language*. It's only taught by a father to his son or a grandfather to his grandson. Girls almost never learn to speak it. Many young Kallawayas don't think they need to learn it so there are only about 20 people who can speak Kallawaya today.

## A WOMAN FIGHTS FOR HER LANGUAGE

Mandarin Chinese is the official language of China now. But in the past, hundreds of different languages and dialects were spoken there. One of these languages is Gelo. Only a few people still speak Gelo but there's one woman who wants to change that. Guo Xiuming is 65 years old. Over the years, she has been collecting information about her language and now she's got a list of more than 70,000 words. Will she be able to save it?

## TWO SPEAKERS WHO AREN'T SPEAKING

There's a language in Mexico that only two people left on Earth can speak. Manuel Segovia and Isidro Velazquez are the last two people alive who speak Ayapaneco fluently. They live only 500 metres from each other but for some reason, they refuse to talk to each other. No one knows why. Some people say, "Maybe they just haven't got much to say to each other."

**15** Read 14 again and answer the questions.

1 Why are there only about 20 people who can speak Kallawaya today?

2 How is Guo Xiuming trying to save her language?

3 Why do Manuel Segovia and Isidro Velazquez refuse to talk to each other?

**THINK BIG** Do you think it's a problem when a language becomes extinct? Why/Why not? What do you think people can do to help save endangered languages?

**16** Read the diary entry.

> Dear Diary,
>
> I'm exhausted today. After I got home, I had to tidy my room,
> do my homework and take the dog for a walk. I can't wait for
> the future when we'll have robots to do everything for us. Nobody will ever
> complain about doing chores again. We won't have any! Robots will tidy up,
> cook and even help us with our homework. So, will I still take my dog for a
> walk? Yes, I'll always do that. Everyone needs to get exercise. But one thing
> will be different. My dog will be a robot, too!
>
> Good night,
>
> Camilla

**17** How does Camilla think her life will be different? Copy and complete the chart.

| Now | Future |
|---|---|
|  |  |
|  |  |
|  |  |

**18** How will your life be different in the future? Write three or four sentences.

**19** Use the information in 18 to write your own diary entry. Share it with a partner.

**THINK BIG** Is it good that life will be different in the future? Why/Why not?

**20** Write four dreams you've got for the future in your notebook. Then compare your dreams with a partner's. Are any of them the same?

> 1 Someday, I'll

> 2 Someday,

> 3 Someday,

> 4 Someday,

**21** Ask and answer with a partner.

1 What's your biggest dream for the future?

2 Why is it important to have dreams for the future?

## PROJECT

**22** Work in a small group. What kinds of products or services will there be in the future? Design an advertisement. Share your advertisement with the class.

# Honey-MOON Hotel

## COME AND SPEND YOUR HOLIDAY IN SPACE!

All rooms have a view of the Earth.
Go hiking on the moon
or relax in our space-spa!

# Listening and Speaking

**2:38**

**23** Listen, read and repeat.

1 p-p  pp    2 b-b  bb    3 d-d  dd

4 m-m  mm    5 n-n  nn    6 t-t  tt

**2:39**

**24** Listen and blend the sounds.

1 h-a-pp-y      happy        2 h-o-bb-y     hobby

3 s-u-mm-er     summer       4 l-a-dd-er    ladder

5 t-e-nn-i-s    tennis       6 b-u-tt-er    butter

**2:40**

**25** Listen and chant.

My favourite hobby
In the summer,
Is playing tennis
And eating bread and butter!

**26** Discuss with a partner. Which of the inventions in this picture of The Future do you think we'll have one day? What other inventions do you think we'll have in the future?

**The Future**

Window, open.

**27** Read and complete.

   **1** In 50 years, people won't use money to buy things.
     Everyone will ?.

   **2** In 100 years, people won't drive cars.
     Everybody will ?.

   **3** In 100 years, we'll have robot teachers and virtual classes.
     No one will ?.

   **4** In 50 years, people won't go to a cinema to watch a film.
     Everyone will ?.

   **5** In 100 years, people will go on holiday to the moon.
     Someone will ?.

**28** Write about two electronic devices that you've got
and what you use them for.

**29** Write about two electronic devices you think you will
have in the future and what you will use them for.

**30** Answer the questions using anyone, everyone, someone or no one.

   **1** Who will use video messaging instead of phone calls in the future?

   **2** Who will use paper and pen to write in 100 years?

   **3** Who will tidy up their bedroom in the future?

   **4** Who will read a book in 100 years?

   **5** Who will ride a bike in the future?

**I Can**

  • **make predictions about the future.**     • **talk about technology.**

## How Well Do I Know It? Can I Use It?

**1** Think about it. Read and draw. Practise.

😊 I know this.     😐 I need more practice.     😟 I don't know this.

| | PAGES | | | |
|---|---|---|---|---|
| **Places to shop:** shopping centre, craft fair, department store… | 43 | 😊 | 😐 | 😟 |
| **Things to buy:** silver earrings, picture frame… | 43 | 😊 | 😐 | 😟 |
| **Holiday-related items:** map, sunglasses, anorak… | 55 | 😊 | 😐 | 😟 |
| **Holiday activities:** kayaking, camping, hiking… | 55 | 😊 | 😐 | 😟 |
| **Electronic devices:** mp3 player, smartphone, tablet… | 67 | 😊 | 😐 | 😟 |
| This camera is **more expensive than** that one.<br>It's **the most expensive** one in the shop.<br>It's **not as expensive as** that one. | 46–47 | 😊 | 😐 | 😟 |
| That helmet is **too** small.<br>Those sunglasses aren't big **enough**. | 46–47 | 😊 | 😐 | 😟 |
| I **was hiking** when it started to rain.<br>I lost my ring while I **was swimming**.<br>**Was** he **cycling** when he fell?<br>Yes, he **was**./No, he **wasn't**. | 58–59 | 😊 | 😐 | 😟 |
| We**'ll use** mobile phones 15 years from now.<br>We **won't have** televisions 15 years from now.<br>Do you think we**'ll drive** cars 100 years from now?<br>Yes, we **will**./No, we **won't**. | 70–71 | 😊 | 😐 | 😟 |
| **Everyone/Everybody** will use email.<br>**No one/Nobody** will use pen and paper. | 70–71 | 😊 | 😐 | 😟 |

## I Can Do It!

**2** Get ready.

2:41

**A** Rewrite the dialogue in the correct order. Then listen and check.

| | |
|---|---|
| **Luke:** | Hey, look at this! |
| **Luke:** | Well, yes, I suppose that's true. Someone should invent sunglasses that you can't lose. |
| **Luke:** | Scientists are working on some amazing new sunglasses. Soon, with these glasses, you'll be able to make phone calls, search for things online, take photos and do all kinds of things! |
| **Luke:** | Really? Why? |
| **Danielle:** | Because I always lose my sunglasses. I lost some last week while I was hiking. And I guess these amazing new glasses will be more expensive than normal sunglasses. |
| **Danielle:** | That sounds like a bad idea to me. |
| **Danielle:** | What? |
| **Danielle:** | Now that sounds like a better idea! |

**B** Practise the dialogue in **A** with a partner.

**C** Ask and answer the questions with a partner.

1 What do you think of sunglasses that work like a smartphone? Are they a good idea or not? Explain.

2 Luke describes two kinds of sunglasses. Which kind would you like to have?

3 Do you think technology will make our lives more interesting in the future or more complicated? Explain.

1

2

3

4

5

6

7

8

9

**3** Get set.

 **STEP 1** Cut out the cards on page 123 of your Activity Book.

 **STEP 2** Arrange the cards facedown in two piles: yellow cards and green cards. Now you're ready to **Go!**

**4** Go!

**A** Pick one card from each pile and make up a sentence following the example.

Last weekend while I was camping, I got a lot of mosquito bites.

**B** Now give advice. What should your partner do differently next time? Then switch roles.

Next time, remember to put on insect repellent!

**5** Write about yourself in your notebook.

- What do you think you'll be doing 20 years from now? Where will you be living? What kind of electronic devices will you be using?
- Which holiday sounds more interesting to you, going to the beach or going camping in the mountains? Why?

## All About Me    Date:_____

_____

_____

### How Well Do I Know It Now?

**6** Look at page 78 and your notebook. Draw again.

A Use a different colour.

B Read and think.

I can start the next unit.

I can ask my teacher for help and then start the next unit.

I can practise and then start the next unit.

**7** Rate this Checkpoint.

 very easy    easy    hard    very hard    fun    OK    not fun

# unit 7

# WHAT'S THAT?

**3:01**

**1** Look at the pictures and read the questions. Choose the correct answers. Then listen and check.

**1** What's this used for?
   **a** giving your hand and wrist a massage
   **b** playing piano music without a piano
   **c** typing messages without a keyboard

**2** What's this used for?
   **a** looking for lost items in a pool
   **b** learning how to swim
   **c** making phone calls in a pool

**3** What's this used for?
   **a** moving quickly underwater
   **b** exploring underwater
   **c** taking pictures underwater

**2** Match the gadgets with words or phrases from the box. Then listen and check.

> **a** mobile phone     **b** handheld game device     **c** hands-free earpiece
> **d** instant camera     **e** transistor radio     **f** video game system

1

2

3

4

5

6

3:03

**3** Listen again. Take notes about each gadget and what it was used for.

| gadget | what it was used for |
|---|---|
| instant camera | to take instant photos |
| | came out in 1948 |
| | was popular in the 70s |

**4** Work with a partner. Ask and answer. Use your notes from 3.

What is it?

It's an instant camera. It was used to take instant photos. It came out in 1948 and it was popular in the 70s.

THINK BIG   Which gadget on this page do you think has changed the most since it was first used? Why?

3:05

**5** Listen and read. What is Mary's necklace worth?

# What's It WORTH?

by Lucy Reynolds

## CAST

Tim, Mary (brother and sister) | Mr Burns (antiques expert)

## SETTING

An indoor antiques market

*[Tim and Mary enter the antiques market. They've got a small dish with them. Mr Burns is sitting at a table with some books about antiques on it. There is a sign on the table that says 'Frederick Burns. Antiques Expert'.]*

**Mary:** *[pointing to the dish Tim is holding]* Excuse me, sir. Could you please look at this for us? It might be worth a lot of money.

**Mr Burns:** *[taking the dish from Tim]* Let's see. What have you got here?

**Tim:** *[shrugging his shoulders]* I'm not sure. We found it in our attic. It was with our great grandmother's things so it's probably quite old.

**Mary:** *[running her hand across the dish]* Do you think it was used for sugar or jam?

*[Mr Burns picks up the dish and examines it carefully. He doesn't seem to be very impressed.]*

**Tim:** Or maybe to hold jewellery? That's what our Aunt Gloria does with her little dish that's just like this one.

**Mr Burns:** Yes, you're both right about how people use these dishes today. But years ago, this kind of dish was used to hold salt. *[He puts the dish on the table.]*

**Mary:** Salt?

**Mr Burns:** Yes. It's probably from the 1930s or so. You see, people used to put salt for each person in these little dishes. After the 1940s, people started to use salt shakers and these little dishes were no longer made.

**Tim:** So are they worth a lot now?

**Mr Burns:** No, not really. This one's in pretty good shape. A dish like it was a very common part of a large set of dishes. If you had the whole set – all the plates, saucers, cups and so on – it might be worth a lot. But for just one little dish, I'd say about £6.

**Tim:** *[disappointed]* I suppose that's why Aunt Gloria just puts her jewellery in it.

**Mr Burns:** *[Mary reaches over to pick up the dish. Mr Burns suddenly notices the necklace Mary is wearing and gasps in surprise.]* My goodness, where did you get that necklace you're wearing?

**Mary:** This necklace? It was in a cardboard box with some old costume jewellery that my mother gave me.

**Mr Burns:** *[in disbelief]* Costume jewellery?

**Mary:** *[trying to clarify]* You know, it's just fake stuff and cheap. Why?

**Mr Burns:** *[examining the necklace more closely]* Well, this is a very rare type of necklace from Venice, in Italy.

**Tim:** Really?

**Mr Burns:** Yes, indeed. And this particular necklace has got a very unusual design.

**Mary:** Uh… what's it worth?

**Mr Burns:** Well, I would say it's worth close to £5,000.

**Tim:** *[shocked]* Five thousand pounds?

*[Mary grabs Tim and starts to run away.]*

**Mr Burns:** *[surprised]* Wait! Where are you going?

**Mary:** *[calling back over her shoulder]* That cardboard box is full of jewellery. I'm going to get it and bring it back here!

**END**

## READING COMPREHENSION

**6** Read and say true or false.

**1** Tim and Mary are at an art show.

**2** They've got a very valuable dish.

**3** The necklace is not just costume jewellery.

**4** Mary and Tim leave to bring back more dishes.

**THINK BIG** Do you think Tim and Mary are glad they took the dish to the antiques market? Why? What makes something that is old, valuable?

**3:07**

**7** Listen and read. What is an abacus used for?

| | |
|---|---|
| **Karen:** | What in the world is this thing? |
| **Thomas:** | I'm not sure. It's one of the weird old things Mr Hartman always brings to class. What do you think it is? |
| **Karen:** | It might be a musical instrument. Or maybe it's some kind of old game or toy! |
| **Thomas:** | It might be. There's Mr Hartman. Let's ask him. |
| **Mr Hartman:** | Oh, hello, you two. What do you think of this abacus? |
| **Thomas:** | This what? |
| **Mr Hartman:** | Abacus. It's used for adding and subtracting. I'm going to show you how to use it in Maths today. |
| **Karen:** | Great! |

**8** Practise the dialogue in 7 with a partner.

**3:08**

**9** Listen and match. Then complete each sentence with the correct form of a verb or verb phrase from the box.

> make butter    ice skate
> sleep          warm beds

**1** It's used for ❓ .

**2** They were used for ❓ .

**3** This was used to ❓ .

**4** It was used for ❓ .

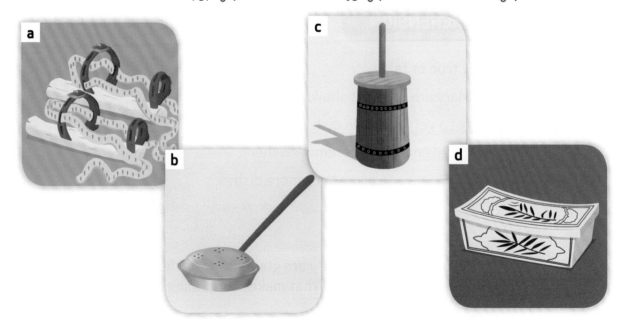

| What's it **used for**? | It's **used for** listening to music. |
| | It's **used to** listen to music. |

**10** Use words and phrases from the boxes to write sentences with used for or used to.

1   _Pans are used for cooking._

2   _____

| glasses |
| a fork |
| headphones |
| pans |

| cook |
| eat |
| listen to music |
| read |

| What is it? | I'm not sure. It **may** be a small plate. |
| | It **might** be a salt dish. |

What **was** it **used for**? Maybe it **was used for** catching fish.

**11** Look at the pictures. What do you think these things are? What do you think they were used for? Make sentences using the words and phrases in the boxes.

| fish trap |
| ice tongs |
| pressure cooker |

| catch fish |
| cook |
| pick up ice |

_It might be a pressure cooker._

_Maybe it was used for cooking._

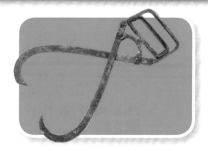

3:10

**12** Listen and read. What were used for lighting before light bulbs?

**CONTENT WORDS**
candle   cash register   combustion engine   fuel   organise   plumbing

# Top Five Inventions

### 1 The Wheel
It all starts here. Wheels are everywhere! They take us to places. They bring things from factories to shops. They're used for operating many kinds of machines. It's hard to imagine life without wheels.

### 2 Indoor Plumbing
Before indoor plumbing, people had to go outside and get water from a pump. You might not think that indoor plumbing is such an important invention. But try to think about all the times you turn on the water in your home every day.

### 3 Light Bulbs
Before light bulbs were invented, candles or oil lamps were used for lighting people's homes. Walk around your home and count how many light bulbs you see. They're everywhere – even inside your fridge!

### 4 Combustion Engine
How will you get to the shops or the cinema? You'll probably go by car, bus or train. If so, you can thank the inventor of the combustion engine. In a combustion engine, fuel burns and makes power. The power from the engine is used for making cars and other vehicles run.

### 5 Computers
You might use a computer to do your homework, organise your schedule or read a magazine. But computers are also used for running things that you use every day. There are tiny computers inside cars, microwave ovens, cash registers in shops and vending machines. It's hard to imagine life without computers – they're everywhere you go.

**13** Read 12 again and match.

1 Wheels are used for    **a** running everyday things.

2 A combustion engine is used for    **b** operating machines.

3 Computers are used for    **c** making vehicles run.

**THINK BIG** Do you agree with the Top Five list? Say why. Make your own Top Ten list. Share your list wih the class.

# COOL TRANSFORMATIONS

**14** Listen and read. How can the shopping bag save your life?

3:11

Designers are very creative people. Look at some common objects that some designers are transforming, or changing, into completely different things.

## The Sound of a Fallen Log

Tree logs are often cut up and used for firewood. Logs are also used for building furniture or even homes. But one company in Austria uses tree logs to make large speakers for mp3 players! An mp3 player connects to a dock on the log and the log has big speakers inside. The hollow log makes the sound better.

log is hollowed out

speakers are mounted on the side

## A Clean Aquarium

Many people like to watch fish in an aquarium. It's very calming and relaxing. People have got aquariums at home, too. But they're usually in a family room or a living room. However, an Italian design company wanted to bring an aquarium into the bathroom and designed an aquarium sink! If you like the sink, this company also sells an aquarium toilet tank!

## A Life-Saving Shopping Bag

Imagine that you're out shopping and there's an earthquake. What do you do? This shopping bag might save your life. That's right. An inventor in Japan is producing these multipurpose bags. The same bag that makes shopping easier can also be used to protect your head! Just empty the bag and turn it upside down. Put it over your head like a hat. The bag is made of the same material as construction helmets.

**15** Read 14 again and answer the questions.

1 Why are the speakers put inside a hollow log?

2 What is unusual about this aquarium?

3 What material is the shopping bag made of?

**16** Read the paragraph describing an invention.

### A Great Invention

This invention is used for finding your way around in the woods or in unfamiliar areas. It's small and round. In fact, it's small enough to fit in your pocket! When you open it, you'll see that it's got a needle. The needle points to the north. This device practically guarantees that you'll never get lost! This important invention is a compass.

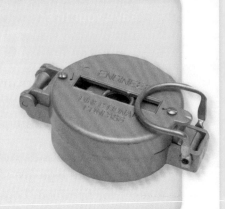

**17** Copy and complete the second column of the chart with details used to describe the invention in 16. Compare with a partner.

| Ways To Describe It | Invention: Compass | My Invention |
|---|---|---|
| What it looks like | small, round | |
| What it's got | | |
| What it's used for | | |
| Why it's important | | |

**18** Write about an invention.

   **A** Choose an invention. Write notes in the third column of your chart.

   **B** Use notes from the chart to write a description of your invention. Don't mention its name until the last line.

**19** Share your description.

   **A** Share your description with the class. Don't read the last line. Ask the class to guess your invention.

   **B** Discuss which inventions you were able to guess and then talk about the new information you learnt.

**20** Work in a small group. Copy and complete the chart, using information you know or can find out about England. If you prefer, choose a different country and create your own chart.

 **ENGLAND**

| People | Places | Events |
| --- | --- | --- |
|  |  |  |
|  |  |  |

**21** Exchange charts with another group. In your group, discuss the other group's chart. For people, places and events you don't know, try guessing. Use may and might to narrow your guesses.

## PROJECT

**22** Create a page for a class book about items that are unique to different cultures.

1 Draw or bring in a picture of an item that is unique to your family's culture.

2 Write what it is, what it's used for and any other information.

3 Put all the pages together to make one book for your class.

This is a piñata. It's used for playing a party game. It's got sweets inside. People wear blindfolds and hit it with a stick. When it breaks open, everyone runs to pick up the sweets!

**THINK BIG** What cultural item in your class book do you find most interesting? Why?

3:12

 **23** Listen, read and repeat.

1 l-t  lt        2 l-k  lk

3 l-d  ld        4 l-b  lb

3:13

 **24** Listen and blend the sounds.

| | | | | | |
|---|---|---|---|---|---|
| **1** | b-e-lt | belt | **2** | m-i-lk | milk |
| **3** | c-o-ld | cold | **4** | b-u-lb | bulb |
| **5** | s-i-lk | silk | **6** | f-ie-ld | field |

3:14

 **25** Listen and chant.

Lets...
Drink cold milk,
Wear a felt belt
And a silk scarf!
And put a green bulb
In the spotlight!

3:15

 **26** Work with a partner. What do you think it is? What was it used for? Use may be or might be in complete sentences. Then listen and check.

1

2

3

4

# Review

**27** Rewrite the sentences in order to form a conversation.

**Kevin:** A package? Oh, good. It may be the new game I ordered.

**Kevin:** Let's see… no, it's too heavy for a computer. Wait. There's a little label here.

**Kevin:** Well, if it is, it looks like and feels like a lot of dog food!

**Alice:** Look! There's a package by the door.

**Alice:** You're right. The label says, 'Canine Power Mix'. Oh, now I remember! I think it might be the new organic dog food for Max!

**Alice:** No, it can't be a game. The box is too big! It might be the computer Dad ordered.

**28** Choose one thing. Write three sentences about what it's used for. Then work in small groups and compare your sentences.

 A (smartphone/computer/watch) is used for...

**29** Work in small groups. Choose items from the class book project on page 91. Write riddles for other groups to guess. Follow the example.

 It's fun to have at a party. It's used to hold sweets.

Is it a piñata?

**I Can**

- guess what things are or might be.

- say what things are used for or used to do.

# unit 8 WHERE DO THEY COME FROM?

3:16

**1** Read and guess where the ideas come from. Write countries from the box. Not all of them will be used. Then listen and check.

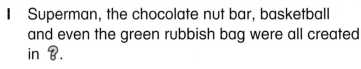

Canada   China   Japan   Norway   the Philippines   the United States

1 Superman, the chocolate nut bar, basketball and even the green rubbish bag were all created in 🤔.

2 CDs, high-speed passenger trains and the cultured pearl were all created in 🤔.

3 Three inventions that make food shopping easier – the automatic door, the shopping trolley and the barcode reader – were invented in 🤔.

4 The world's first karaoke machine was made in 🤔.

5 What became the first aerosol spray can was developed in 🤔.

**2** Read the list of products. What are they made of? List them. Some can be listed more than once. Then listen and check.

| PRODUCTS | |
|---|---|
| blankets | scarves |
| boots | cola cans |
| floors | cookers |
| flower pots | jumpers |
| planes | tyres |
| plates | towels |
| rugs | T-shirts |

**1** These things are made of **cotton**.

**2** These things are made of **rubber**.

**3** These things are made of **metal**.

**4** These things are made of **wool**.

**5** These things are made of **clay**.

3:18

**3** Listen. Where do the materials come from? Match. Two materials come from the same place. Listen again and check.

**1** Rubber comes from      **a** animals like sheep.

**2** Metal comes from      **b** the Earth's crust.

**3** Cotton comes from      **c** a plant.

**4** Wool comes from      **d** a liquid found in trees.

**5** Clay comes from

**4** Ask and answer.

What material are rugs, towels and T-shirts made of?

They're made of cotton.

**THINK BIG** What do you think is the most important material? Why?

**5** Listen and read. Where was pizza first made?

www.travelfans.com

| | |
|---|---|
| **travelbug** | Help! My family and I are thinking about going to Italy for a holiday. We've only got five days to spend there so we can't see everything. Where should we go? |
| **castle_hopper** | Hi, travelbug. You should definitely come to Tuscany. There's so much to do here and everything is close by. Florence is the capital of Tuscany. It's known for its beautiful palaces, churches and other buildings. Many of the most famous works of Renaissance art can be found here in the museums and galleries. You could spend five days just looking at the art in Florence!<br><br>Siena is a beautiful medieval town. It's filled with incredible old buildings. If you've got time, go to the Palio de Siena, a medieval horse race that's held twice a year. It's attended by thousands of people so be prepared! |

Florence

Palio de Siena

| | |
|---|---|
| **seat1A_flyer** | Hey, travelbug! If this is your first trip to Italy, you should definitely see Rome. This city is known for some of the most famous sites in the world: the Colosseum, the Pantheon, the Spanish Steps… the list goes on and on! Vatican City, the smallest country in the world, is located inside Rome, too. And you can't leave Rome without seeing the ceiling of the Sistine Chapel. The ceiling was painted by Michelangelo and is *amazing*!<br><br>If you're in Rome, you could easily go on a quick trip down to Naples. It's been called the birthplace of pizza; and is located on the beautiful Amalfi Coast. So you can enjoy your pizza while you sit and look out at the sea! |

Colosseum

Vatican City

**getaway_gary73** Ciao, travelbug. Rome and Tuscany are nice but for something really unique, try Venice. Venice is known around the world as a floating city. Most of its 'streets' are filled with water! They're called canals. To get around Venice, you can take a water taxi.

Some of the most beautiful buildings in the world were built in Venice. There's the Piazza San Marco – a beautiful city square next to St Mark's Cathedral. This site is visited by thousands of people every year. You can find some unique souvenirs here, too. You could get a necklace made of Murano glass. Or you could buy one of those famous masks from the Venice Carnival. The masks are known around the world. They're worn during celebrations at Carnival time here. Venice really is an incredible place.

Venice

Piazza San Marco

## READING COMPREHENSION

**6** Read and say true or false.

1 Tuscany is the capital of France.

2 The medieval horse race is held twice a month in Siena.

3 The ceiling painted by Michelangelo is located in Rome.

4 Venice is often called the birthplace of pizza.

5 Most streets of Venice are crowded with cars.

6 Murano glass is produced in Venice.

**THINK BIG** Why do you think Italy is visited by millions of people each year? Which place in Italy would you like to visit? Why?

**7** Listen and read. What new information does Sue find out about Costa Rica?

**Martin:** I can't wait. We're going to Costa Rica next week!

**Sue:** Costa Rica? I don't know much about that country.

**Martin:** Well, you've come to the expert! What do you know about it?

**Sue:** I know that it's in Central America.

**Martin:** It is! But can you guess what it's known for? A third of the country is made up of them.

**Sue:** I haven't got a clue.

**Martin:** Its rainforests! A lot of agricultural products come from there, too. In fact, that banana you're eating was probably grown there.

**Sue:** This banana? How do you know?

**Martin:** Read the sticker on it.

**Sue:** Costa Rica… you're so clever!

**8** Practise the dialogue in 7 with a partner.

**9** Listen and match. Then complete the labels with words from the box.

China   Hungary   Morocco   Saudi Arabia

**1** Made in 🔍   **2** Made in 🔍   **3** Made in 🔍   **4** Made in 🔍

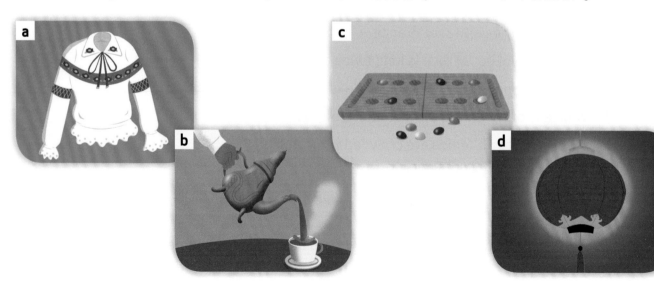

| That watch **is made** in Switzerland. | The first pizza **was** probably **made** in Italy. |
| Those bananas **are grown** in Ecuador. | The first noodles **were** probably **made** in China. |

**Tip:** To form the passive, use the present simple or past simple form of the verb *be* with the past participle of the main verb.

**10** Put the words in order to make statements.

1  Switzerland/in/made/watches/are

2  bananas/in/Ecuador/are/grown

3  was/the/made/pizza/first/Italy/in

4  the/were/noodles/first/China/in/made

5  in/strawberries/grown/are/England

6  first/bar/the/Canada/chocolate/made/was/in

**11** Make sentences. Use the present simple passive form of the verb in brackets.

1  Sheep ❓          (raise in/China)

2  Diamonds ❓      (mine in/Africa)

3  Pottery ❓        (make in/Italy)

4  Coffee ❓         (export from/Costa Rica)

5  Rubber ❓         (produce in/Brazil)

**12** Complete the sentences. Use the past simple passive form of the correct verb from the box.

design     eat     import     sell

1  Millions of mobile phones ❓ in Japan last year.

2  This video game ❓ in Spain.

3  A lot of pizza ❓ in Britain last year.

4  All the flowers in this market ❓ from Holland.

3:25

**13** Listen and read. Who should you buy fresh produce from?

> **CONTENT WORDS**
> diesel fuel    distribution centre    local    pollution    produce    typical

## From the FARM to Your PLATE

Imagine you're at a restaurant. You order a salad. When it comes, it looks delicious. You can't wait to take that first bite. But stop for a moment and think about how long it actually took to get to your plate. Not from the kitchen but from the farm.

As an example, let's take a look at a typical salad served in the United Kingdom. Nowadays, most foods eaten here travel thousands of kilometres before they get from the farm to the shop. 'Fresh' foods, such as the lettuce in a typical salad, may be grown locally. But other foods are grown far away, even halfway around the world. These foods have to be washed, packed and brought to a distribution centre before they make their way to a shop. So your salad may not be so 'fresh' after all!

All forms of transport involved with shipping foods and other goods cause air pollution. The farther food travels, the more petrol and diesel fuel are used. The more petrol and diesel fuel are used, the more pollution is released into the air we breathe. Shipping fresh produce can add up to 45 times more pollution to the air. So eating healthy foods is not always a healthy thing to do.

There is a solution, however. Fresh produce can be bought from local farmers. The lettuce that was picked yesterday will taste a lot better and will be better for you than the lettuce that was picked a week ago. So try to buy fresh, local produce as much as possible!

Do you shop at your local farmers' market or fresh produce stand? If not, before ordering another salad, ask where the produce was grown. You'll be able to tell what is fresh!

**14** Read 13 again and match.

1 distribution centre     a poisonous fumes

2 produce     b place from where things are delivered

3 pollution     c foodstuffs

**THINK BIG** Does food have to travel far where you live?
Is it better to have food you like all year round, no matter how far it travels? Or is it better just to eat what's local and in season? Why/Why not?

**15** Listen and read. Did early Chinese judges wear sunglasses?

# Where Did It Come From?

Do chips, or French fries, come from France? Actually, most people believe they were first made in Belgium, not France. Do you ever wonder where other foods or products come from?

**JIGSAW PUZZLES** In 1767 in England, John Spilsbury wanted to teach his pupils geography. He glued a map of England and Wales to a flat piece of wood. Then he cut out the map along county borders. Each county was one piece of wood. After mixing up the pieces, his pupils put the map puzzle back together. Back then, the pieces did not lock together. The jigsaw puzzles we see today were invented about 100 years later, after power tools were invented.

**SPAGHETTI** The Chinese have been making noodles since 3000 BC, well before Italians. The explorer Marco Polo brought noodles to Europe from the Far East in the 13th century. This became spaghetti! Thomas Jefferson took some of this pasta to the United States from France in the 1700s.

**MATCHES** An Englishman named Robert Boyle found a new way to make fire. He mixed the chemicals phosphorus and sulphur together. A little over a century later, in 1827, another Englishman named John Walker used the combination of these two chemicals to create the first matches. The matches were one metre long!

**FRIDGES** Refrigeration is a way of making things cold so they stay fresh. Refrigeration uses special gases to do this. A German engineer named Carl von Linde found out how to make this work. Linde built his first fridge in a factory in Dublin, Ireland, in 1894.

**SUNGLASSES** For centuries, early Chinese judges wore smoke-coloured glasses. But these weren't sunglasses – they were used to hide the judges' eyes in court so no one could guess what they were thinking!

**16** Copy the chart into your notebook and complete.

| | What? | Who? | When? |
|---|---|---|---|
| **1** | Spaghetti | ? | 13th century |
| **2** | ? | John Walker | 1827 |
| **3** | Fridges | Carl von Linde | ? |

**17** Read the paragraph. Find the main opinion. Note down three reasons used to support it. Do the reasons persuade you to visit Corsica? Discuss with a partner.

## Come to Sunny Corsica!

main opinion →

This beautiful island paradise, a territory of France, is located in the beautiful Mediterranean. It's made up mostly of mountains, which run from north to south in a single chain. The coast, however, offers vast stretches of fabulous beaches. It's the perfect place for a family holiday! The main languages spoken here are French and English, making it easy to find out everything you need to know. The island is known for its hiking in spectacular mountainous scenery. It's also popular for diving along its unspoilt and wild shoreline. But, if you want a less active holiday, Corsica is also the perfect place for sunning yourself on one of its magnificent beaches. The island's rich history makes it perfect for those wanting culture, too! Come and visit Corsica and find out firsthand why it's known for being a top holiday destination!

**18** Choose your favourite holiday spot. Write a topic sentence expressing your main opinion. Write three reasons.

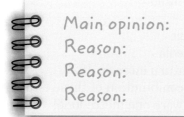

> Main opinion:
> Reason:
> Reason:
> Reason:

**19** Use the information you listed in 18 to write a paragraph.

**20** Exchange paragraphs with your partner. Did your partner's reasons persuade you?

> **THINK BIG** Why does travel writing try to persuade people?
> What other examples of writing that tries to persuade people can you think of?

**21** Copy and complete the chart for each category. Follow the examples. Then discuss with a partner.

| What I appreciate | Where it comes from |
|---|---|
| The food I eat<br>*fruit like oranges*<br>*salad* | *right here in Spain*<br>*local markets and right in my garden* |
| The clothes I wear | |
| The transport I use | |
| The technology I use | |

**22** Work in small groups. Compare your charts. Do you appreciate some of the same things?

> I like my jeans. They're made of cotton from China.

**PROJECT**

**23** Choose a category from the chart in 21. Draw or find pictures to make a poster. Label where each comes from. Give a presentation about your poster.

I appreciate my clothes
Made in China
Made in India
Made in Italy
Made in Turkey

**3:27**

**24** Listen, read and repeat.

1 l-f   lf      2 l-p   lp      3 l - m   lm

**3:28**

**25** Listen and blend the sounds.

1 g-o-lf      golf          2 h-e-lp      help
3 f-i-lm      film          4 e-lf        elf
5 e-lm        elm

**3:29**

**26** Listen and chant.

School clubs are fun clubs!
Golf clubs,
Film clubs
And best of all,
Help Others clubs!

**27** Work in small groups. Talk about places you know and what they are known for.

1 Write the names of the places on slips of paper.

2 Write what the places are famous for or known for on other slips of paper.

3 Put the slips into separate bags – one labelled 'Place' and the other labelled 'What It's Known For'.

4 Work with another group. Swap bags.

5 Take turns drawing slips of paper and guessing the place or what it's known for.

6 Continue until all are guessed or revealed.

Oranges are grown here.

Is it Spain?

**28** What are they made of? Use words from the box.

> clay   cotton   metal   rubber   wool

1   Flower pots, plates and floors are made of ❓.
2   Cola cans and planes are made of ❓.
3   Tyres and boots are made of ❓.
4   Warm winter jumpers are made of ❓.
5   Most T-shirts and sheets are made of ❓.

**29** Make sentences using the present simple passive form of the verbs.

1   coffee/grow/in Kenya
2   cattle/raise/in Argentina
3   glass beads/make/in Venice
4   cotton/produce/on special farms around the world
5   grapes/grow/in France

**30** Make sentences using the past simple passive form of the verbs.

1   the chocolate nut bar/create/Canada
2   the shopping trolley/invent/the United States
3   the first patented karaoke machine/make/the Philippines
4   high speed passenger trains/create/Japan
5   the first aerosol spray can/develop/Norway

## I Can

- **talk about where goods come from.**
- **talk about products and the materials used to make them.**
- **use the passive voice.**

# unit 9

# HOW ADVENTUROUS ARE YOU?

**4:07**

**1** Have you ever wondered about the food you eat? Read the fun facts about food. Guess the correct answers. Then listen and check.

**1** Refried beans are fried ?.

  **a** twice

  **b** once

  **c** three or more times

**2** The first soup was probably ?.

  **a** hot vegetable soup

  **b** cold fruit soup

  **c** hippopotamus soup

**3** The ingredient that makes one popular junk food pop in your mouth is ?.

  **a** just air

  **b** carbon dioxide

  **c** sugar

**4** Ice cream is actually ?.

  **a** Indian food

  **b** Italian food

  **c** Chinese food

**5** Blueberries ?.

  **a** may help your memory

  **b** may help your hearing

  **c** may cause permanent tooth discolouration

**2** Choose two adjectives from the box to describe each food. Then listen and check.

| cold | delicious | different | good | hot | popular | pretty | raw |
|------|-----------|-----------|------|-----|---------|--------|-----|
| sour | spicy | sweet | tasty | terrible | traditional | unusual | wonderful |

**Soup from Spain**

**Soup from China**

**Japanese Appetiser**

**Greek Appetiser**

**Moroccan Dish**

**Indian Dish**

**Italian Dessert**

**Philippine Dessert**

**3** Point to the foods in 2. Ask and answer with a partner.

Would you rather try the cold soup or the hot soup?

I haven't eaten cold soup before! I'll try it. What's it called?

It's called gazpacho. It's very popular in Spain!

I love it! It's delicious.

**THINK BIG** What traditional foods do you know? Can you describe their taste? How adventurous are you about food? Is it good to be adventurous about food? Why/Why not?

**4:05**

Listen and read. Where is 'ugali' a local food?

# HIGH ADVENTURE *at* HIGH ALTITUDES

**by Phil Steadman**

**Explorer Gilda Navarro updates us on her attempt to climb the Seven Summits – the highest mountain on each of the world's seven continents.**

**Phil Steadman:** Good morning, Gilda. Thanks so much for talking to us today. I know you're busy preparing for your next mountain adventure.

**Gilda Navarro:** Of course, Phil. It's always a pleasure. I could use a break, anyway!

**Phil:** You certainly have been busy over the last two years.

**Gilda:** Yes, you could say that!

**Phil:** For our listeners who may not know, over the last two years you've climbed six of the world's seven tallest mountains. That's amazing for such a short period of time. I get tired just thinking about it!

**Gilda:** My dad always says I've got a lot of energy.

**Phil:** That's certainly true! When we last spoke, you were getting ready to climb Mount Kilimanjaro, in Africa. What was it like?

**Gilda:** That was a great one. Well, they've all been great. Mount Kilimanjaro isn't the highest of the Seven Summits. It's actually number four. It's 5,895 metres high and it's located in Tanzania.

**Phil:** I see. How long did it take you to climb it?

**Gilda:** It took me and my team a full seven days to climb that one.

**Phil:** Wow. What did you eat during the climb? Was it local Tanzanian food?

**Gilda:** Not really. We had pasta, rice dishes… normal things.

**Phil:** So the food wasn't as adventurous as the climb, was it?

**Gilda:** Oh, we had a lot of delicious local food after we got back. There's a tasty Tanzanian food called ugali. Have you ever heard of it?

**Phil:** No, I haven't. Is it spicy?

**Gilda:** No, ugali is quite plain by itself. It's made of corn. It looks a little like mashed potatoes. You roll up some ugali in a ball and you dip it in stew.

**Phil:** That sounds like good comfort food.

**Gilda:** Yes, I've tried different kinds of food everywhere. I'm pretty adventurous about food, I think.

**Phil:** What about your next climb?

**Gilda:** We're getting ready for our last mountain. And we've saved the best for last.

**Phil:** Mount Everest?

**Gilda:** That's right. It'll take us a few weeks to climb Everest.

**Phil:** Is that because it's so high?

**Gilda:** Well, yes. To climb Mount Everest, you have to stop at several different places and let your body get used to the altitude. If you don't, you'll be in big trouble!

**Phil:** I bet! I've got one more question. Imagine you had to choose from one of these: going mountain climbing or going on an all-expenses-paid trip to a gorgeous tropical beach. Which one would you rather do?

**Gilda:** That's the world's easiest question. I'd rather go mountain climbing! There's nothing better.

**Phil:** Spoken like a true adventurer! Gilda, thank you for spending time with us. Good luck with that last summit.

**Gilda:** Thanks so much. It was fun talking to you.

## READING COMPREHENSION

**5** Read and say true or false.

1 Gilda Navarro has climbed the world's seven highest mountains.

2 Mount Kilimanjaro took Gilda less than a week to climb.

3 Gilda and her group ate local Tanzanian food after their climb.

4 Mount Everest takes weeks to climb to allow time for adjustment to the altitude.

**THINK BIG** How do you feel about Gilda's attitude to climbing?
Would you ever want to climb a mountain? Why/Why not?
What would you like to ask Gilda about what she has done?

**6** Listen and read. Why is Abigail *really* going to go to the concert with her dad?

**Dad:** Abigail, there's a concert down at the Arts Centre this weekend. Do you want to go?

**Abigail:** What kind of concert?

**Dad:** It's classical music. You know… Mozart, Beethoven.

**Abigail:** Classical music? Uh, no thanks. I'd rather stay at home.

**Dad:** Come on! Have you ever been to a classical music concert?

**Abigail:** Well, no… I haven't. But I don't think I'd like it.

**Dad:** That's a pity because the Arts Centre is giving free BoysTown concert tickets to the first 25 people who come that night.

**Abigail:** What? The BoysTown concert? I think I've changed my mind.

**Dad:** Oh, really? Why?

**Abigail:** Well, Dad, I've never been to a classical music concert before. I might like it. Let's make sure we get there early, OK?

**7** Practise the dialogue in 6 with a partner.

**8** Listen and match. Then complete the sentences with the correct form of the verb from the box.

> be    learn how    study    try

**1** Jason has never ⚡ to skateboard.

**2** Claire has never ⚡ to a water park.

**3** Sally has never ⚡ Thai food.

**4** Allie has never ⚡ another language.

| | |
|---|---|
| **Have** you ever **been** to a concert? | Yes, I **have**./No, I **haven't**. |
| **Has** he ever **been** skydiving? | Yes, he **has**./No, he **hasn't**. |

**9** Complete the questions. Then make answers.

1 Have you ever 🕮 a horror film? (see)

2 Have you ever 🕮 skydiving? (be)

3 Have you ever 🕮 on a stage? (perform)

4 Have you ever 🕮 sushi? (eat)

| | |
|---|---|
| **Would** they **rather** play football or watch it? | They'**d rather** play football. |

**10** Look at the survey. Complete the questions. Use would and rather. Then make answers.

1 🕮 play video games or go skateboarding?

2 🕮 write a story or play chess?

3 🕮 visit a museum or create a sculpture?

4 🕮 go fishing or bake a cake?

## Pupil Interest Survey

Dear Pupil,
We're putting together an after-school programme and we want
your input! Please tick all activities that interest you. Thanks!

Name: *Chloe Harrison*

| | | | |
|---|---|---|---|
| ☐ Baking | ☑ Sculpture | ☐ Chess | ☐ Video game competition |
| ☑ Short story writing | ☑ Fishing | ☑ Skate-boarding | ☐ Visiting museums |

**4:10**

**11** Listen and read. What does adrenalin do to your body?

> **CONTENT WORDS**
> adrenal glands    adrenalin    cells    heart
> hormone    lungs    release    stress

# Adrenalin:
# FIGHT OR FLIGHT

Have you ever watched a scary film and felt like your heart was going to jump out of your chest? If so, then you were probably feeling the effects of adrenalin.

What is adrenalin? Adrenalin is a hormone made by your body. Hormones give important messages to different cells in your body. When you get scared – for any reason – your body sends out adrenalin. When this happens, your whole body gets ready to fight something scary or to run away from it. That's why adrenalin is sometimes called the 'fight-or-flight' hormone.

The release of adrenalin in your body gives you an extra boost of energy. Blood rushes to your muscles so your heart starts beating quickly. Air moves rapidly into your lungs so you start taking short, fast breaths of air. These are normal reactions to fear or stress and it happens to everyone.

The force of adrenalin going through your body is designed to help you. There have been many stories about people who have used 'superhuman' strength in order to save another person's life. In most cases, though, the effect is not so dramatic. For example, imagine you are riding on your bike and suddenly someone steps out in front of you. Quick! What do you do? Your brain makes a fast decision to get out of the way and the release of adrenalin helps make your body move quickly.

So next time you ride a rollercoaster, watch a scary film or get nervous before a race, pay attention to how your body reacts. You'll probably feel the effects of adrenalin at work.

> Adrenalin gets into your cells from your adrenal glands, located at the top of your kidneys.

**12** Read 11 again and say true or false.

1 Adrenalin is also known as the 'fight-or-flight' hormone.

2 When adrenalin is released into your body, your heart beats less quickly.

3 'Superhuman' strength is caused by adrenalin in the body.

**13** Listen and read. What is an aerialist?

# High Adventure!

Some people take extreme risks and love doing it. Others don't even want to think about doing such dangerous things.

## Cliff Diving in Mexico

Have you ever jumped into a pool from a diving board? Most diving boards are about 1 metre above the pool. Competitive divers dive off boards that are even higher than that. They dive off 3-metre and 10-metre diving boards. Some people find that scary. But how about diving off the side of a cliff? The La Quebrada Cliff Divers are professional, trained cliff divers. They dive into the sea from 38 metres above – head first.

## BASE Jumping in Norway

Have you ever wanted to fly? BASE jumping is just like flying but it's very dangerous, even for trained professionals. Trained BASE jumpers begin by standing at the top of a very high place, like a mountain, and then jump down, using a parachute to slow down their fall. BASE stands for Buildings, Antennas, Spans (bridges) and Earth (cliffs). The Troll Wall in Norway is one of the highest points in Europe – 1,700 metres high. Because it's difficult to rescue people from it, BASE jumping is no longer allowed there.

## Tightrope Walking in Niagara Falls

The Flying Wallenda Family is a family of aerialists who travel all over the world doing tricks high up in the air. In 2012, Nik Wallenda did a tightrope walk across Niagara Falls, between the United States and Canada on a tightrope that was only 5 centimetres wide. It took him 25 minutes. On 23rd June, 2013, Nik walked across the Grand Canyon – live on TV! What's next? He wants to walk between two pyramids in Egypt.

**14** Read 13 again and complete.

1 Cliff divers dive off the 🤔 of a cliff.

2 BASE jumpers jump from a high place and use a 🤔 to slow their fall.

3 🤔 do tricks high up in the air.

**THINK BIG** Which of these activities sound the riskiest to you? Why?
Which of these activities would you like to watch or try? Why?

**15** Read the paragraph, then copy and complete the chart about it.

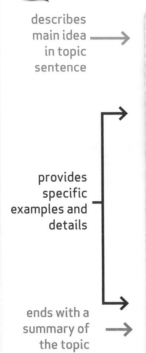

describes main idea in topic sentence →

provides specific examples and details

ends with a summary of the topic →

> I'm a pretty adventurous person in some ways. I love to hike and enjoy hiking on new trails. However, I have always been afraid of heights. This is something that I'm trying to change about myself because in the future I want to hike up a mountain and mountains are high! To challenge myself, I've been on the highest rollercoasters at the local amusement parks. They were scary but fun! Also, last year when I went to Paris, I went on the tour that takes you up to the top of the Eiffel Tower. It was a bit scary, too but the view from the top was amazing! I may not like heights but I do like adventures. And I know one day I'll lose my fear of heights and I'll go and climb that mountain!
>
> – by Stella

| How Stella is adventurous and willing to try new things – challenges |
|---|
| Example: |
| Example: |

**16** Now choose two ways you are adventurous and willing to try new things from the box. Use them to write a descriptive paragraph about yourself.

Clothes
Challenges
Food
Hobbies
Making New Friends
New Places

**17** Share your descriptions with the class. Who is the most adventurous?

**THINK BIG** Is it good to be adventurous? Why/Why not?

**18** Answer the questions in your notebook. Then interview a partner and record the answers.

| Have you ever...? | Me | | My Partner | |
|---|---|---|---|---|
| | Yes | No | Yes | No |
| been to an art show at a local museum | | | | |
| danced at a local festival or celebration | | | | |
| helped clean up an area in your community | | | | |
| seen or talked to the mayor of your town | | | | |
| volunteered to work with younger children | | | | |
| visited a local farm | | | | |
| attended a concert or film at a local park | | | | |
| had a picnic at a local park | | | | |
| been swimming at a public beach or pool | | | | |
| visited someone at a nearby care home | | | | |
| been to a sports event at another school | | | | |
| been hiking or camping near where you live | | | | |

## PROJECT

**19** Find photos to make a collage of the things you could explore in your community.

In my community, there are many parks and a lake, too. I've never fished in it but I've been swimming there. I plan to visit a local farm. I've visited a care home and plan to do it again soon!

**20** 4:12

Listen, read and repeat.

**1** f -t    ft      **2** c -t    ct

**3** m-p    mp      **4** s-k    sk

**21** 4:13

Listen and blend the sounds.

**1** l-e-f-t      left       **2** f-a-c-t      fact

**3** c-a-m-p    camp     **4** r-i-s-k      risk

**5** r-a-f-t      raft       **6** l-a-m-p     lamp

**22** 4:14

Listen and chant.

> It's a fact that
> Sailing at night
> On a raft,
> Without a lamp,
> Is a risk!

**23** Do a survey. On your own, complete each question in your notebook by writing two activities. Then work in groups of four. Take turns asking your questions. Record the answers.

Would you rather go on a rollercoaster or ride a horse?

I'd rather ride a horse. Rollercoasters scare me!

| Would you rather... ? | Pupil 1 | Pupil 2 | Pupil 3 |
|---|---|---|---|
| go on a rollercoaster<br>or<br>ride a horse | | | |
| or | | | |

**24** In your group, ask and answer about the activities in your survey.

Have you ever ridden a horse?

No, I haven't. But I'd like to try.

**25** Complete the sentences with the words from the box. Then answer the questions.

delicious    spicy    terrible    traditional    unusual

Last night, my family tried a new restaurant in the city. It serves ¹ 🐾 Indian food. My older sister thought the food was too ² 🐾 and started to cough. My brother thought it was so ³ 🐾 that he ordered more. My little sister thought it was ⁴ 🐾 and asked for a cheese sandwich. My Aunt Millie tried a dessert that she'd never had before. She said it was very ⁵ 🐾 but she would order it again.

1  Would her older sister rather eat more or have a glass of water?

2  Would her brother rather not come back or come back often?

3  Would her little sister rather have more Indian food or have something else to eat?

4  Would her aunt rather try another dessert or have the same one again?

**26** Answer the questions. Add a sentence that gives additional information.

1  Have you ever eaten Indian food?

2  Have you ever tried a new food and loved it?

3  Have you ever made dinner at home for your family?

4  Have you ever climbed a mountain?

5  Have you ever been on a rollercoaster?

6  Have you ever dived off a cliff?

**I Can**

• talk about experiences.

• talk about preferences.

## How Well Do I Know It? Can I Use It?

**1** Think about it. Read and draw. Practise.

😊 I know this.    😐 I need more practice.    😟 I don't know this.

| | PAGES | | | |
|---|---|---|---|---|
| **Electronic devices (old and new):** transistor radio, video game system, mobile phone… | 83 | 😊 | 😐 | 😟 |
| **Materials:** rubber, wool, cotton… | 95 | 😊 | 😐 | 😟 |
| **Products:** blankets, tyres, T-shirts… | 95 | 😊 | 😐 | 😟 |
| **Adjectives:** delicious, spicy, unusual… | 107 | 😊 | 😐 | 😟 |
| What**'s** it **used for**? It**'s used for** reading. What **were** they **used for**? They **were used to** carry big things. | 86-87 | 😊 | 😐 | 😟 |
| It **may** be a mirror. It **might** be something for cooking. | 86-87 | 😊 | 😐 | 😟 |
| That bracelet **is made** in Switzerland. The first noodles **were** probably **made** in China. | 98-99 | 😊 | 😐 | 😟 |
| **Have** you ever **tried** raw fish? Yes, I **have**./No, I **haven't**. | 110-111 | 😊 | 😐 | 😟 |
| **Would** you **rather** go hiking or stay at home? I**'d rather** go hiking. I**'d rather not** stay at home. | 110-111 | 😊 | 😐 | 😟 |

## I Can Do It!

4:15

**2** Get ready.

**A** Complete the dialogue using the statements from the box. Then listen and check.

> a I've had it before.
>
> b It's known for its spicy flavours.
>
> c I'd rather try something new tonight.
>
> d I've never had Korean food.
>
> e Some of them are made out of metal.

**Dad:** Hi, Madeline. What kind of restaurant would you rather go to tonight – Polish or Korean?

**Madeline:** I don't know. I've tried Polish food but ¹ [?] .

**Dad:** Oh, really? ² [?] .

**Madeline:** What's it like?

**Dad:** It's delicious. ³ [?] . And it usually comes with rice.

**Madeline:** Sounds interesting. Do you use chopsticks to eat it?

**Dad:** Yes, a lot of Korean dishes are eaten with both chopsticks and a spoon. But Korean chopsticks are different from other ones.

**Madeline:** In what way?

**Dad:** ⁴ [?] .

**Madeline:** Really? That's interesting, too.

**Dad:** So… what do you think – Polish or Korean?

**Madeline:** ⁵ [?] . Let's go to the Korean place!

**B** Practise the dialogue in **A** with a partner.

**C** Ask and answer the questions with a partner.

1 Have you ever tried Polish food or Korean food?

2 How adventurous are you with new foods? Explain.

3 What's the most unusual food you've ever tried? What was it made of? Would you like to have it again? Why/Why not?

1
2
3
4
5
6
7
8
9

**3** Get set.

 **STEP 1** Cut out the cards on page 125 of your Activity Book.

 **STEP 2** Put the cards facedown and mix them up. Now you're ready to **Go!**

**4** Go!

**A** Game 1

Work in a small group. Take turns. The first pupil turns over one card. Ask the people in your group.

Have you ever played in a chess tournament?

**POINTS:**

If no one says *Yes*, keep the card.

If one person says *Yes*, give the card to him/her.

If more than one person says Y*es*, ask: *When?* The person who did it first gets the card.

Continue until the cards are gone.

Try to be the person with the most cards at the end.

**B** Game 2

First, match each card to the card that has the same beginning word. Then take turns asking questions. When you answer, give a reason.

Would you rather write a short story or an apology email for something you did wrong?

I'd rather write an apology email for something I did wrong. Writing a short story sounds hard to me.

**C** Tell the class about some of the choices and reasons from your group.

**5** Write about yourself in your notebook.

- What's the most adventurous thing you have ever done? Did you enjoy it? Why/Why not?

- Describe an unusual object you've seen before. Where's it from? What's it made of? What's it used for?

# All About Me

Date:_____

_____

_____

## How Well Do I Know It Now?

**6** Look at page 118 and your notebook. Draw again.

A Use a different colour.

B Read and think.

I can ask my teacher for help.

I can practise.

**7** Rate this Checkpoint.

very easy    easy    hard    very hard    fun    OK    not fun

1
2
3
4
5
6
7
8
9

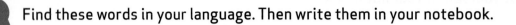

Find these words in your language. Then write them in your notebook.

| Unit 1 | Page | Unit 2 | Page | Unit 3 | Page |
|---|---|---|---|---|---|
| act | 2 | be born | 15 | advertisement | 32 |
| analyse | 8 | celebrate | 21 | animal rescue | 33 |
| art club | 4 | decorate | 21 | benefit (v.) | 33 |
| athletics team | 4 | find/get a job | 19 | charity groups | 33 |
| basketball team | 3 | get married | 15 | design posters | 27 |
| brain | 8 | graduate | 15 | design | 32 |
| build robots | 3 | holiday | 21 | donate | 26 |
| competition | 9 | move | 15 | effective | 32 |
| control | 8 | offspring | 20 | font | 32 |
| creative | 8 | open a restaurant | 15 | have a cake sale | 27 |
| do martial arts | 12 | predator | 20 | have a concert | 27 |
| drama club | 3 | protect | 20 | have a dance | 28 |
| football team | 4 | retire | 16 | have an art fair | 27 |
| instructions | 8 | special | 21 | homeless | 33 |
| jog | 3 | traditions | 21 | images | 32 |
| medals | 9 | wedding | 21 | layout | 32 |
| metres | 9 | young (n.) | 20 | make a video | 27 |
| Olympic Games | 9 | | | make something | 28 |
| paint | 4 | | | post a video/article on | |
| personality | 8 | | | the school website | 27 |
| play chess | 3 | | | raise money | 26 |
| play sports | 3 | | | sell tickets | 29 |
| play the trumpet | 3 | | | tutoring | 33 |
| race course | 9 | | | write an article | 27 |
| school newspaper | 3 | | | | |
| school orchestra | 3 | | | | |
| school play | 5 | | | | |
| science club | 3 | | | | |
| solve | 8 | | | | |
| sporting events | 9 | | | | |
| tae kwon do club | 3 | | | | |
| write articles | 13 | | | | |

| Base Form | Past Simple | Base Form | Past Simple | Base Form | Past Simple |
|---|---|---|---|---|---|
| ask | asked | help | helped | sing | sang |
| bake | baked | hit | hit | sit | sat |
| be | was/were | hold | held | skateboard | skateboarded |
| begin | began | hope | hoped | sleep | slept |
| bring | brought | keep | kept | snowboard | snowboarded |
| build | built | kill | killed | speak | spoke |
| buy | bought | know | knew | stand | stood |
| call | called | learn | learnt | start | started |
| catch | caught | leave | left | stay up | stayed up |
| celebrate | celebrated | like | liked | swim | swam |
| change | changed | listen | listened | take | took |
| come | came | live | lived | talk | talked |
| cook | cooked | look | looked | tell | told |
| cut | cut | lose | lost | think | thought |
| destroy | destroyed | love | loved | throw | threw |
| do | did | make | made | travel | travelled |
| draw | drew | meet | met | try | tried |
| drink | drank | move | moved | turn | turned |
| drive | drove | need | needed | understand | understood |
| eat | ate | perform | performed | use | used |
| explain | explained | plan | planned | visit | visited |
| fall | fell | play | played | wait | waited |
| feed | fed | put | put | wake up | woke up |
| feel | felt | read | read | walk | walked |
| fight | fought | realise | realised | want | wanted |
| find | found | rest | rested | wash | washed |
| fly | flew | ride | rode | watch | watched |
| get | got | ring | rang | wear | wore |
| give | gave | run | ran | worry | worried |
| go | went | say | said | write | wrote |
| grow | grew | see | saw | yell | yelled |
| have | had | sell | sold | | |
| hear | heard | send | sent | | |

**Education Limited**
.........ourgh Gate
**Harlow**
**Essex CM20 2JE**
**England**
**and Associated Companies throughout the world.**

www.pearsonelt.com/bigenglish

© Pearson Education Limited 2014

First published 2014
Ninth impression 2018

ISBN: 978-1-4479-5130-8

Set in Apex Sans
Editorial and design management by Hyphen S.A.
Printed in Slovakia by Neografia

### Acknowledgements

The publisher would like to thank the following for their contributions:
Tessa Lochowski for the stories and CLIL pages.
Sagrario Salaberri for the Phonics pages.

The publisher would like to thank the following for their kind permission to reproduce photographs:

(Key: b-bottom; c-centre; l-left; r-right; t-top)

**Alamy Images:** AlamyCelebrity 66t, amana images inc 70t, 115cl, Anatoliy Cherkasov 2-3 (background), 38br, Aurora Photos 61cr, B Christopher 37t, Bubbles Photolibrary 55 (c), Creative Control 50, Dennis MacDonald 61b, Frankie Angel 83/4, GOIMAGES 83/2, 118 (below centre), Anthony Hatley 33c, Image Source 54t, 78t, imagebroker 9tl, Janine Wiedel Photolibrary 3/6, Jonah Calinawan 107 (Moroccan), Judy Freilicher 22, Lana Rastro 15 (b), Lee-Ann Wylie 113b, LOOK Die Bildagentur der Fotografen GmbH 42t, Lynden Pioneer Museum 87bl, MARKA 30, 96tr, Iain Masterton 42br, mediacolor's 110b, Mira 4b, i (centre left), Morgan Lane Photography 34t, Myrleen Pearson 33b, 39, 55 (h), Patti McConville 25b, Peter Phipp / Travelshots.com 49b, Simon Price 59, 78 (below centre), Sinibomb Images 31, 83/6, Steve Vidler 49t, Stocktrek Images, Inc 72c, Tetra Images 98l, Yulia Kuznetsova 26br; **Corbis:** Google / Handout 66bl, Ocean 3/3; **DK Images:** Dave King, Andy Crawford 92/3, Karen Trist 87br, Susanna Price 18, Robert Schweizer 61cl; **Fotolia. com:** 2tun 43 (bracelet), Aaron Amat 92/4, Adrian 97l, Africa Studio 43 (balloons), alarsonphoto 43 (earrings), 78 (above centre), alessandrozocc 88/2, andersphoto 100 (lettuce), Andrey Kuzmin 100 (knife & fork), Anibal Trejo 104t, arinahabich 114, arquiplay77 95/3, Arto 2c, Artur Synenko 48c, asese 8r, i (left), 38t (centre), AVAVA 77, Barbara Helgason 43 (frame), Beatrice Prève 4t, biker3 75, bkhphoto 63c, bondsza 2b, BVDC 15 (d), Canadeez 66br, chris2766 91tl, Chrispo 101cl, Claudio Divizia 48b, 78bl, Frédéric COIGNOT 97r, Cybrain 94tr, Darrin Henry

33t, Denis Pepin 28, Denys Prykhodov 66bc, dja65 92/1, DM7 74, DmitriK 21c, Douglas Knight 9tr, 38bl, duckman76 2t, EJ White 11r, 27bl, 83br, 104br, 115 (boy), Elenathewise 101b, emese73 8l, EpicStockMedia 54-55 (background), eurobanks 94br, Fotokon 48t, Gelpi 3bl, 34br, 43bl, 67bl, 93bl, 95br, germanskydive110 111t, GoodMood Photo 95/1, Haslam Photography 43 (roses), Herjua 14t, higyou 72b, hitdelight 101t, Igor Klimov 67/2, 78bc, iofoto 58t, Jacek Chabraszewski 26l, JJAVA 106t, 107 (Indian), 118t, Joe Gough 117, JonMilnes 82/3, Julián Rovagnati 111b, Kadmy 25/1, kaphotokevm1 25/4, 38t, KaYann 96tl, Ken Hurst 7bl, 11l, 15bl, 116br, Beatrice Kesseler 102, Kzenon 14br, Lisa F. Young 19, 27tc, littleny 14bl, mast3r 27tr, MasterLu 96br, Meliha Gojak 101cr, Michael Flippo 51, micromonkey 9b, milachka 7, Milos Tasic 95/2, 118 (above centre), mirabella 43 (necklace), Mitchell Knapton 55 (g), Monkey Business 3/2, 6, i (centre), 55 (a), 115bl, Natalia Danecker 106b, Nathan Allred 15 (c), olesiabilkei 95/4, paylessimages 89b, percent 95/5, petunyia 55 (d), plutofrosti 67/4, Robert Lerich 107 (Greek), romikmk 106c, Scanrail 94bl, 118 (train), SerrNovik 103b, sframe 105, Simone van den Berg 26tr, skynet 99, soundsnaps 83/3, stockcreations 106 (background), strelov 92/2, sumnersgraphicsinc 94tl, tarei 20tr, Tombaky 29, tr3gi 88/1, tuja66 83/1, Tupungato 103t, Ulrich Müller 100t, volgariver 96bl, WANG HSIU-HUA 60bl, WINIKI 89t, zagorskid 66c; **Getty Images:** Ben Speck & Karin Ananiassen 73t, Terence Langendoen / The Image Bank 55 (f), uwe umstätter 86 (boy & girl), Yoshikazu Tsuno / AFP 82/1; **Glow Images:** Aurora Open / Henry Georgi 54l, Blend RF / Hill Street Studios 14c, Bridge / Jim Cummins / CORBIS 3/4, i (right), Bridge / Laureen Morgane / Corbis 54b, 63t, Caroline Mowry / Somos Images / Corbis 88/5, ImageBroker / Ulrich Doering 3/1, NordicPhotos / Svenne Nordlov 27tl, PhotoNonStop / Eurasia Press 49c, Purestock 23b, Uppercut RF / Jerry Marks Productions 15 (a); **Newscom:** Jaime Avalos / EFE 73b, JP5\ZOB / WENN.com 82/2, Lin Bin / Xinhua / Photoshot 73c, Splash News / Opulent Items 89c; **Pearson Education Ltd:** Jon Barlow 27br, 52l, 67b (centre left), 83bl, 104bl, 107bl, Gareth Boden 43br, 52r, 91br, 95bl, 98r, 116tl; **Photo Researchers, Inc.:** Dante Fenolio / Science Source 20tl; **PhotoEdit Inc.:** Jeff Greenberg / PhotoEdit 37b; **Photoshot Holdings Limited:** C. C. Lockwood 20b; **Rex Features:** MOBA 61t; **Shutterstock.com:** 3Dstock 67/1, 71b, Andresr 23t, Antonio V. Oquias 107 (Philippine), AVAVA i (centre right), 67br, baitong333 60t, bonchan 107 (Spain), C Salisbury 44 (camouflage), Carlos Caetano 13, Jacek Chabraszewski 42bl, 78br, charles taylor 10, Cherkas 44b, Daniel Padavona 107 (Italian), Danny Smythe 64, Elena Elisseeva 60 (background), Elena Schweitzer 42-43, Elzbieta Sekowska 115br, 118b, ESTUDI M6 113t, eurobanks 3br, 7br, 15br, 34bl, 67b (centre right), 93br, 116tr, 116bl, Feng Yu 89 (bag), FERNANDO BLANCO CALZADA 67/3, fet 3/5, fotohunter 21b, HomeStudio 86 (abacus), ifong 106-107, Ivonne Wierink 32, 38b (centre), Jason Winter 83 (background), Jeff Banke 60br, JHDT Stock Images LLC 107br, Looper 15 (banner), marekuliasz 45, marylooo 21 (background), MaszaS 55 (e), MaxyM 115cr, Melanie DeFazio 25/3, Michael J Thompson 90, Michelle Eadie 108-109, Mike Heywood 70b, Mikhail Zahranichny 55 (i), Monkey Business Images 1l, 110t, Nata-Lia 44t, Natali Glado 47, Norman Chan 107 (China), Ociacia 72t, Oleksandr Chub 83/5, Patrick Breig 71t, Peter Zvonar 88/3, quetton 61 (background), Robert Kneschke 25/2, rprongjai 107 (Japanese), Rudy Balasko 88/4, Sebastian Kaulitzki 112, Renata Sedmakova 91tr, Sharon Day 87t, SUSAN LEGGETT 55 (b), Tom Hirtreiter 63b, Tomasz Trojanowski 46, vrvalerian 89 (background), Ysbrand Cosijn 21t; **SuperStock:** Exactostock 58b, Fancy Collection 1c, imagebroker. net 1cl, Radius 1cr, Stockbroker 1r